Out to Change the World

The Evolution of The Farm Community

Douglas Stevenson

Book Publishing Company
Summertown, Tennessee

Library of Congress Cataloging-in-Publication Data

Stevenson, Douglas, 1953–
Out to change the world : the evolution of The Farm community / Douglas Stevenson.
pages cm
ISBN 978-1-57067-303-0 (pbk.) — ISBN 978-1-57067-891-2 (e-book)
1. Communal living—Tennessee—History. 2. Collective settlements—Tennessee—History. 3. Farms—Tennessee—History. I. Title.
HQ971.5.T2S74 2014
307.77'409768—dc23

2014003379

Book Publishing Company is a member of Green Press Initiative. We chose to print this title on paper with 100% postconsumer recycled content, processed without chlorine, which saves the following natural resources:

33 trees
993 pounds of solid waste
15,098 gallons of water
2,722 pounds of greenhouse gases
14 million BTU of energy

For more information on Green Press Initiative, visit greenpressinitiative.org.

Environmental impact estimates were made using the Environmental Defense Fund Paper Calculator. For more information, visit papercalculator.org.

Cover and interior design: Karen Sandorf
Stock Photography: Shutterstock

Printed in the United States

Book Publishing Company
PO Box 99
Summertown, TN 38483
888-260-8458
bookpubco.com

ISBN: 978-1-57067-303-0
19 18 17 16 15 14 1 2 3 4 5 6 7 8 9

Photo Credits

Pages 6, 7, 12, 15, 23, 38, and 43: © Book Publishing Company

Page 149: courtesy of Cayanne Ramuten Stevenson

Pages v, 65, 68, 81, 107, 131, and 151: courtesy of Douglas Stevenson

Pages 81, 82, and 88: courtesy of Plenty International

Cover photo and pages 21, 35, 41, 47, 50, 55, 95, 96, 101 (top), and 101 (bottom): © The Foundation

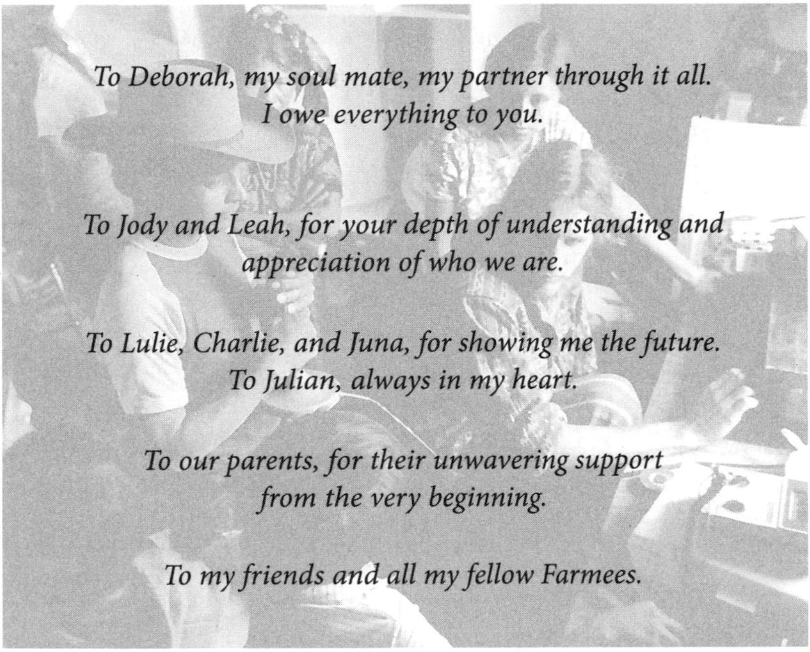

To Deborah, my soul mate, my partner through it all.
I owe everything to you.

To Jody and Leah, for your depth of understanding and appreciation of who we are.

To Lulie, Charlie, and Juna, for showing me the future.
To Julian, always in my heart.

To our parents, for their unwavering support from the very beginning.

To my friends and all my fellow Farmees.

Contents

Preface

Deborah, Douglas, and baby Jody on The Farm, 1974.

I have invested virtually all of my adult life in The Farm community. I say "invested" because I have put everything I have both materially and spiritually into it, and reaped the fruits of these efforts a hundredfold.

My wife, Deborah, and I came to The Farm in 1973, two years after the original group landed with the bus Caravan in 1971. We were both nineteen, married almost two years, and together since we were fifteen. When we arrived we were the youngest couple on The Farm.

I remember feeling that we were late to the party. We had missed the Summer of Love in San Francisco, and by the time we got to The Farm, there were already about four hundred people in the community. Now looking back over the last forty years, we have seen so much of the community's history pass before our eyes and have been very active participants through it all.

As it turns out, 1973 was probably a good time to arrive. Those of us joining the community that year had less of our psyche invested in Stephen Gaskin as a spiritual teacher and guru. As a result, at least from my observation, more of us who arrived at that time made it through the community's power shift and turmoil of the early 1980s, and have remained in the community to this day. I didn't want to be "head copped," that is to say brainwashed, into blindly following anyone, even though I did accept Stephen as a spiritual teacher. To me he was our spokesperson and a figurehead, passing on knowledge and teachings through words and example. I really didn't have a personal, one-on-one conversation with him for my first seven years with the community.

Very early on I expressed that I believed the real spiritual teacher was the community itself, with every individual committed to self-improvement by endeavoring to follow universal spiritual truths. Stephen brought these truths to our attention and awareness through his weekly sermons on Sunday, which were also transcribed, edited, and put out as books. The community, or more correctly the people you lived with, the people you worked with, were the ones who got to see the real you and would get on your case, pointing out your ego, your mistakes, and the ways you were falling short of our collective ideals. This is how you changed and grew as a person.

Our son was born in 1974 with the help of The Farm Midwives. In the late fall of that year, when our son was just a few months old, Deborah and I moved to a smaller, satellite community in Kentucky, called The Green River Farm, which started out with just one other family and grew to about twenty-five folks over the course of our two years there. During our second summer at Green River Farm, we went back to Tennessee for several months for the delivery of our second child, a daughter.

After our return, in the fall of 1975, the Kentucky group collectively decided to sell that land and a bunch of us went to another satellite Farm in upstate New York. Deborah and I stayed there for a few months and in the spring moved back to Tennessee. By the next fall we were ready for something new and went down to spend the winter at The Florida Farm, which was actually more of a city center. Come spring we went back up to Tennessee.

In the fall of 1978, we moved once again to experience the adventure of a lifetime, working with Plenty, The Farm's new nonprofit that was managing relief projects in Guatemala. I can only describe our time there as a peak life experience, and it forever changed my view of the world. Our return to Tennessee in September of 1980 was not entirely by choice. It was brought about by the dangerous political climate in Guatemala after the election of Ronald Reagan as US president, whose policies led to a brutal repression in which hundreds of thousands of Mayan people were killed and millions more became refugees in their own country and along the border with Mexico.

Things were a bit different when we returned to The Farm this time. The population had swelled to around fifteen hundred people, but the infrastructure and income needed to support that many people just wasn't there. By the fall of 1983, the communal system collapsed under its own weight. Over the next several years, there was a steady exodus until only 100 adults and 150 kids remained. We were among those who stayed.

I started a small business. Deborah went back to school to become a registered nurse and graduated first in her class. She also received training and became one of The Farm Midwives. The kids grew up and started their lives as adults.

In the meantime, over the next several decades, I got more involved in the community, serving four years (two terms) on its membership committee, six years (two terms) on its board of directors, and eight years as community manager. I took on the tasks of public relations and interfacing with press and media. A natural extrovert, I have always used my gift of music to provide entertainment, starting with the communal households of the 1970s. Even more importantly, once the communal period came to an end, I used music as part of the glue to hold the community together, performing in bands, organizing festivals, and keeping alive our annual tribal reunion.

Starting around the turn of the century, I began developing retreats, workshops, and conferences wrapped in the various themes of community and sustainability as a way to encourage others to follow their dreams. Community provides a richness of experience that is unparalleled, deeply intertwining work and play, family and friends, joys and sorrows.

I have tried to tell our story as accurately as possible to the best of my knowledge. In the early days of The Farm, I was not part of the "inner sanctum," or engaged in the higher levels of management. I was a worker bee like thousands of others who came to The Farm to be a part of something bigger than ourselves, to follow a spiritual path, to make a difference in the world.

It has been a very full life. I am honored to share The Farm's story, and my story, with you.

ONE

Prelude to the Sixties

To understand the creation of The Farm as an intentional, spiritual community, one has to take in a broad overview looking back through history at previous experiments in collectivity and communal living. It's important to also acknowledge the gradual influx of Eastern philosophies into North America and the societal shifts taking place in the United States during the 1940s and 1950s, which led to the cultural revolution of the 1960s and the wake of its aftermath. The combination of all these new ideas contributed to the circumstances that generated the spark that brought The Farm to life. Although hundreds of other alternative-lifestyle communities have become established or are on the brink of conception, The Farm remains a true product of its times, reflecting the values that coalesced during the peak of the hippie influence.

Communal Societies

Scholars who study communal societies are quick to point out that the early Christian monasteries and Eastern ashrams were some of the first examples of intentional communities, created by people who chose to join together in order to pursue a specific spiritual path. These groups often supported themselves through small commercial enterprises and cared for their own needs, such as producing food and raising livestock.

During the mid to late 1800s, a broad array of social living experiments were taking place within the United States. These communal societies lasted from a few years to several decades. Some groups followed charismatic leaders, while others practiced unique spiritual disciplines that were often based on an interpretation of Christianity. There were also communal societies that attempted to address broad social issues, such as racism and slavery, breaking away from conventional society to establish new moral values of equality.

However, the difficulties these communities faced eventually did them in. They dissolved, and the people involved with them were integrated into the surrounding communities.

East Meets West: Gurus and Spiritual Teachers

The early 1900s saw the first wave of New Age mysticism migrate from East to West, with Indian gurus such as Meher Baba and Krishnamurti acquiring large followings of dedicated seekers, especially among a segment of the wealthy. Although these Eastern teachers were virtually unknown to the majority of people in the Western world, they were sufficiently supported by this small group of devotees for them to publish books, establish centers, and pursue successful lecture tours in both Europe and the United States during the ensuing decades.

One of the most successful New Age philosophers came not from India or Asia but from Germany. In the late 1800s, Rudolf Steiner's anthroposophy delivered a blend of Christianity and cosmic consciousness that spread from Europe to America and around the world. Many of Steiner's teachings developed into well-established models that remain with us today, from Waldorf education to biodynamic farming. Steiner's unique approach to the treatment of mental illness and education, along with encouraging social integration and respect for people with physical deformities, continues in the form of intentional communities dedicated to this service. These communities still flourish around the world, including in numerous locations throughout the United States.

Political Awareness

This wave of spirituality in the early 1900s paralleled another significant philosophical trail in society—the growing political awareness among workers as expressed through unions, as well as socialist and communist agendas. Once again this coincided with a continual call for greater racial equality and the advancement of women's suffrage, and for voting rights for both groups.

The atomic bombs dropped in World War II represented such tremendous power for destruction and world annihilation that they inspired broadscale national and international peace and antiwar movements. "Ban the Bomb" became the slogan to counter the insanity of "duck and cover," the useless exercises in preparedness foisted on the country's schoolchildren. More often than not, those carrying the antiwar banner were members of Christian faiths, such as the Quakers, who already had a long-established history of conscientious objection and refraining from military service.

The Beats

By the 1950s, the Beat Generation pushed these cracks in society a bit wider, dropping out of the mainstream in search of greater meaning and higher consciousness and challenging the status quo. This was happening at the same time that Jack Kerouac went on the road, Elvis and Chuck Berry energized rock and roll, and James Dean became the *Rebel Without a Cause*. Rosa Parks, Martin Luther King Jr., the Birmingham bus strike, and the undeniable moral strength of the civil rights movement provided meaning and a call to action: Young people picked up on the outrage against the establishment that was churning throughout the nation. All of these movements in music, popular culture, and activism set a tone for the emergence of the hippies in the 1960s. Young, middle-class white kids found their voice through Pete Seeger, Bob Dylan, and the folk music ethos of peace, love, and understanding. It became clear that "the times they were a changing," with millions of young people coming of age, unwilling to follow their parents into what they saw as the drudgery of factory work or corporate careers.

It was this strength in numbers that served as a catalyst for change on a variety of fronts. The nightly TV news delivered the reality of the Vietnam War and the racism of the South, while other media shined a light on the new wave of sexual liberation. The joy and freedom experienced through rock bands, such as the Beatles, the Rolling Stones, Buffalo Springfield, and countless others helped galvanize the energy and ideals of the emerging boomer demographic.

By the mid-1960s, children born just after the end of World War II were old enough to leave home. As word began to filter east about the excitement happening on the West Coast, and specifically in San Francisco, thousands upon thousands of young people heeded the call and poured into the city like a human tidal wave. The mild temperatures of the Bay Area made it relatively easy to survive, so that a new vagabond needed little more to join the blossoming flower power movement than a bowl of brown rice and a corner to crash in someone's apartment.

TWO

San Francisco, Monday Night Class, and The Caravan

San Francisco became a symbol and focal point for changes that were taking place all around the world. Young people were questioning and challenging the established order, as they so often do. But at perhaps no other time in history had this taken place on such a large scale. New ideas, questioning the status quo, gained traction quickly in this youth culture. The shared language of rock music, and a burgeoning attention by the media, sped the message to eager ears.

Be Sure to Wear Some Flowers in Your Hair

All across the country, word began to filter out that something was happening on the West Coast. Psychedelic rock performed by such bands as Jefferson Airplane and Santana dominated the music floating on the national airwaves. Alternative media and underground newspapers, such as the *San Francisco Oracle*, were full of stories describing the scene in San Francisco, making it appear very attractive, especially for young people tuned in to the cultural shift but feeling lost and smothered by the conservative values of America's heartland. In a replay of the original gold rush, those seeking a new way of life packed up and headed west. Covered wagons were replaced by old station wagons and VW vans on a cross-country trek, driving east to west until they reached California.

The summer of 1967 will forever be known as the Summer of Love. The bliss was fueled by what can only be called a shared religious experience, an unbelievable explosion of expanded consciousness brought about by the ingestion of LSD. Swept up in that wave was one unlikely character, a former Marine turned university professor.

Stephen Gaskin

Stephen was born in 1935, putting him just ahead of the actual baby boomers. By 1966, he had served with the Marines in Korea, married and divorced, totaled a sports car, and taken a position teaching creative writing at San Francisco State University.

A former marine and Berkeley University creative writing teacher, Stephen Gaskin became a fixture of the Haight-Ashbury scene when he began hosting a weekly forum called Monday Night Class in 1970.

Stephen spoke about his time at San Francisco State: "I remember I was teaching one of my first freshman English classes, and the stuff my students were giving me to read was just trash. It was just terrible. I said, 'You guys are treating me like I'm your ninety-year-old aunt, and I'm going to die if anybody says anything heavy to me. This next paper you're not going to be graded on grammar, you're not going to be graded on spelling. You're going to be graded on whether you have anything to say.'

"And the stories I got back were dynamite—heavy personal stuff, like a (white) girl working it out with her mother over whether she was going to be able to keep her black baby; real things in their lives. I thought to myself that if I followed the regular school format, I'd never get to know any of this. I wouldn't get to know who they were. That class made me realize that although I loved the kids deeply, the university was just a pain in the butt."

Stephen felt he understood the cultural revolution of the time, but he learned otherwise. One of his students politely told him that although he was fun and kind of cool, he really didn't have a clue about what was going on. He decided to find out.

Coming down from the hills of higher learning to the scene on Haight Street was a definite eye-opener. The intense energy generated by the scores of young people immediately captivated Stephen. "There was an undeniable buzz happening that you could feel to the center of your bones," he said.

Changes on the inside were also reflected on the outside. Like most other young men of the day, Stephen began to grow his hair long. Soon a wispy beard sprouted from his chin.

As fate would have it, the president of San Francisco State at the time was none other than S. I. Hayakawa, a future right-wing senator of California, well known for his hard line toward the antiestablishment rhetoric expressed by students of the day. As fall came around, it was time for Stephen's teaching contract to be renewed. He returned to campus after months immersed in the free-spirited Summer of Love. He trimmed his hair, put on a suit, and then waltzed into Hayakawa's office, announcing with a smug curtsy, "Is this square enough for you?" The short answer was no.

"I didn't get fired for being weird; I just got too weird to be rehired by the time my contract ended," Stephen recalled with a sly grin. And just like that, Stephen was out of a job and set free to pursue his destiny.

"I had no idea what I was going to do," Stephen said.

Monday Night Class

Campuses at most of the liberal colleges across the United States experimented with the Free University, an attempt to provide students with an outlet for creative expression within the accepted confines of traditional education. Essentially, that meant teachers, professors, and others were permitted access to classroom space after hours to hold classes on non-accredited subjects.

Monday Night Class attracted up to 2,000 people a week, hippie visionaries seeking a better understanding of life and the universe.

"I didn't want to move off campus. San Francisco State was one of the centers of the hippie culture," Stephen explained. "I realized I wanted to keep talking to these young people, and so I went to the experimental college guy. He said there was an opening Monday nights. I said I'll take it. The first meeting had a dozen people. The next, only six. It took me a year to get up to a hundred."

Stephen and his handful of students began gathering weekly to hold discussions. Their meetings could be described as sessions in which they compared notes, endeavoring to gain a better understanding of their shift in consciousness. For many, including Stephen, it was a new awareness, a new dimension they had rocketed into by way of the LSD experience. With the doors of perception blown wide open, the weekly class began examining a range of philosophical genres. Class titles such as "North

American White Witchcraft" and "Metaphysical Education" give a hint at what was up for discussion. Stephen introduced the writings of sages through the ages, as well as modern philosophers, such as Aldous Huxley and Alan Watts. Esoteric spiritual teachings, Eastern religions and disciplines, and even the mainstream doctrines of Christianity and Judaism all seemed to share the same threads of truth. What's more, these truths resounded as honest expressions of universal life lessons when viewed through the new lens of the psychedelic experience. Along with the peace and love came moral values: honesty, compassion, and—going one step further—justice.

One of the most significant teachings borrowed from Eastern philosophy was the expression of "karma," the cause and effect of one's actions. Under the influence of psychedelics, karma could be felt instantaneously. This perceived psychic wisdom illustrated how people's levels of awareness could be understood through their actions, whether they were expressions of love or anger. Even subtle thoughts of others were easily detected by those in highly sensitive mental states as changes in vibrations. Perhaps the greatest revelation was that these feelings and sensitivities remained present even after the psychedelic high was over. In short, life was a trip, and the journey was guided by taking personal responsibility for one's actions, attitude, and energy. This was the essence of Stephen's message.

Over the next year, word of Stephen and the weekly discussion spread. He offered a forum to the thousands of young people in the Bay Area who were eager to gain a greater understanding of the mysteries they'd glimpsed through the magic of the psychedelic experience. As the class grew, larger venues were required to contain the hordes of spiritual seekers.

By 1970, the weekly meeting, now known as Monday Night Class, had grown to as many as two thousand people. Leveraging his previous experience as college professor, Stephen had settled into the role of spiritual teacher. His was a uniquely American version, in contrast with the numerous Eastern gurus in the area. Stephen became a fixture on the Haight-Ashbury scene, well known and sometimes chided for his principles. The song "St. Stephen" by Jerry Garcia of the Grateful Dead was never publicly acknowledged to be written about Stephen, but it describes a character referred to as "The Answer Man," who many of the band's fans and residents of the Haight took to be a tongue-in-cheek reference to the Bay Area's counterculture guru.

The Monday Night Class meetings became a testing ground for ideas and energy perception. The group learned how to deal with minor distractions, such as crying babies and wandering dogs. Stephen would open the meeting with an "Om," a single shared tone created by each person's pure voice, said to represent the sound of the universe. This would quiet everything down, and when it was over, there was a hushed silence in the room. After a bit, Stephen would begin to talk. In general, people were very respectful of the shared energy. Stephen would address the crowd without a microphone, using nothing more than the power of his voice. There were also times when it would get raucous, and there might be someone in the crowd who was a little nutty, who would just start hollering, or the occasional loudmouthed heckler. Stephen learned how to run the meeting, maintaining a sense of control and order so the group wouldn't get out of hand.

To complete his immersion into hippie culture, Stephen peppered the language of his talks with a plethora of New Age and hippie jargon, even at times making up his own phrases and adding them to the mix. For example, this dialogue from Monday Night Class about the truth was no doubt understood by the audience of the day, but a bit of translation can be useful for its meaning to be fully comprehended.

Stephen: "There are very funny things that can happen about words. Words are very, very heavy magic. Everything you say is true, on some level. You only think you can lie, but you can't really. If you tell a lie on the material plane, your astral will cop on you."

Translation: Nonverbal communication, a person's body language and energy, points to the truth.

"You see? If there's anybody paying attention, you can't lie," Stephen taught. "You can only lie to people who don't feel vibes. But anybody who feels vibes—when someone's telling a lie, it makes a certain vibration, and it says, 'lie.'"

The hippie movement was divided into two camps: spiritual seekers and political activists, with most people falling somewhere in the middle. Hard-core leftists dismissed spirituality as more opiate for the masses and called for active, even violent struggle against the establishment. Several factors led to this call for a more aggressive stance. The draft remained a threat to young men all across the country, as the Vietnam War was a continual looming presence. The emergence of more militant groups, such as the Black Panthers and Students for a Democratic

Society, commanded more attention in the media and among fellow antiestablishment groups, all seeking to instigate significant social change. The murder of pacifist Martin Luther King Jr., followed by the assassination of antiwar presidential candidate Robert F. Kennedy, left many on the left feeling that the nonviolent approach was ineffective.

The debate came to a head at Monday Night Class following the 1970 massacre at Kent State University in Ohio, where National Guardsmen opened fire on peaceful protesters, killing four Kent State students and wounding several more. Seething with anger and frustration, representatives of the more radical political element in the class challenged Stephen's nonviolent stance and called for armed struggle.

The debate was loud and contentious, but Stephen held firm. Most of the more dedicated members of the class lined up in support of nonviolence, and by the end of the meeting there was clear agreement. Everybody understood; more violence was not the answer.

The Minister Convention

During the summer of 1970, San Francisco played host to a national convention of Christian ministers, meeting to discuss the proverbial generation gap that was dividing parents and their children, personified by the hippies. The ministers could clearly see the disillusionment young people had with Christian faiths and that their flocks were shrinking. To gain a better understanding of the hippie lifestyle and its effect on American youth, the group listened to presentations by a variety of speakers. Stephen was the only person they heard who represented the voice of the hippie movement directly. All others were mere observers who could offer no more insight than their own observations.

"I was the only hippie who got to address them," said Stephen, describing the meeting. "They had the doctor from the Haight Street free clinic. They had cops. They had psychiatrists. But I was the only actual hippie." Stephen took the ministers by surprise when he honored them for following a spiritual calling and gave them respect for the path they had chosen. Stephen went on to tell the ministers, "What we have here is a spiritual void, so you're already in the right business." Needless to say, he made quite an impression, and he was very well received.

Stephen presented a few obvious truths about the hypocrisy of the church, such as its support for war, which clearly contradicted the message of Jesus, who had spoken unequivocally about loving your neighbor and turning the other cheek. How were they able to rationalize the absolute disregard for the biblical commandment "Thou shalt not kill"?

Stephen understood that the church sought to forge a stronger connection with young people. He recognized that he could serve as a more relevant spiritual advisor to those on the voyage from youth to adulthood—a period of soul searching and a quest for the meaning of life—and that his teaching might be able to have more influence on the young than that of the church. Stephen believed that until organized religion could reconcile its own shortcomings, it would not capture new youthful adherents. Only those who did not choose to think for themselves could be expected to follow the church without question.

Stephen's influence was undeniable. A few weeks after the convention, some of the church representatives made contact and asked Stephen if he would consider going on a speaking tour, making stops at churches all across the country.

The idea intrigued him, and as it happened, the proposed tour would coincide with the release of *Monday Night Class*, a book containing edited transcriptions of Stephen's talks and lectures. A national speaking tour would provide an excellent way for Stephen to promote the book. On the next Monday night, Stephen announced that class would be suspended and go on recess until after his return.

To save money on rent, Stephen and his extended immediate family, which by that time included several children, had moved into a school bus converted into a house trailer of sorts, complete with beds and a small kitchen, an early prototype of the RV. In order to make the space more accommodating for Stephen, who stood over six feet tall, the roof of the bus had been cut out with a welding torch and raised up an extra two feet, creating a homemade double-decker. The plan was to take the bus on tour from west to east and back again.

By this time many of the young people attending the weekly meetings had become regulars and were developing a more personal relationship with Stephen. Now in his midthirties, Stephen was at least ten years older than most of his hippie followers. This gap in maturity helped solidify his role as spiritual advisor, even father figure. Not ready for the separation and unhappy with this new turn of events, many of those at Monday Night Class grew excited about the idea of an extended road trip. They relished the notion of sharing their revelations and newly discovered spiritual truths with fellow hippie brothers and sisters across the country. The question was put to Stephen: "Can we come too?"

The Caravan

The next month was spent getting ready. Additional buses were purchased from up and down the West Coast, vintage vehicles from the 1940s and '50s that could be had for as little as a few hundred dollars. Seats were removed and the interiors renovated; some buses were outfitted to house groups of ten or more. Small rectangles of woven mats, carpet samples in a former life, were glued to the interior roofs and became a common design theme, adding a patchwork of color and softening the impact of tall heads bumping up against the low ceilings. It was also hoped that this would provide some measure of insulation from the cold. Since the route would take them across the Northwest in the middle of winter, small woodstoves were installed in some of the vehicles as well.

The Caravan departed from San Francisco with dozens of school buses and over 200 people.

The Caravan departed from San Francisco in August of 1970 with about sixty buses and an assortment of converted bread vans, delivery trucks, a station wagon, and a few cars. It was agreed that each bus would have its top painted white to project a unified presence, but the rest of the bus bodies were painted in a variety of colorful hues and designs so that no one would mistake them for real school vehicles. The buses were given names to reflect various themes, from the origin of the owners (The Sausalito Bus) to the names of the drivers (Wilbur and Karen's) to playful descriptions (Cadillac Camper) to clever phrases of alliteration (The Freeway Flier).

The Caravan had been on the road for only a night and a day when it appeared that the entire escapade would be halted in its tracks.

"When we got up to the California-Oregon border, suddenly a hundred flashing red lights went off," Stephen said. "They had cops from all the surrounding states, sheriffs from all the surrounding counties, the FBI, federal narcotics agents." Officers entered the lead bus, driven by Stephen, and said, "We have orders to arrest the registered owner of this bus." Much to their surprise, that wasn't Stephen.

The cops left and then came back a few minutes later. "We have orders to arrest Stephen Gaskin." Stephen was escorted to jail. A collection was taken up and a short time later Stephen was bailed out with a handkerchief full of nickels, dimes, quarters, ones, and fives—much to the chagrin of the authorities.

Standing before the court, Stephen proclaimed, "We are the peaceful people, who are peaceful about being for peace." He further explained that he was on a lecture tour with a schedule of appointments, and that he would be speaking at churches across the country. This caught the judge by surprise, and he made a ruling that set the history of The Farm in motion.

The judge granted Stephen bail, setting his court date for later the following year. Stephen recalls the judge saying, "I'll tell you what I'll do. I'm going to let you go on your speaking tour. You'll come back here at the end of it, and we'll know what you were all about." Stephen was free to go.

In many ways, The Caravan was a dose of reality for these American middle-class kids. They found themselves completely unprepared for what they would face on the road. Stephen was fond of saying that it turned out college students' summer jobs were more important than their college majors.

It was no small feat to keep sixty vintage school buses running. Right away, it became necessary to learn everything there was to know about combustion engines and all of the support systems needed to keep a vehicle on the road.

"We had one guy who knew mechanics and another who would say a prayer over your carburetor," Stephen recalled with a smile.

Pushed to new extremes, sometimes the old engines would give up. The hard truth was that The Caravan had a schedule to keep, and if you wanted to stay with the group, you had to keep your bus ready to roll. There were times when serious mechanical difficulties would prevent a bus from driving on with the group. Once repairs were made, that bus would drive double-time to catch up with The Caravan somewhere down the road.

Buses need fuel, and fuel costs money. While there were a few people along for the ride who had money to share, the intention was for The Caravan to pay its own way. This meant that when the buses arrived in a new town, representatives went out to seek any kind of paying work they could find. Without any practical skills, the best they could hope for was basic manual labor, what many people might consider menial tasks. The effort provided a direct correlation between work and reaping the fruit of your labor. Money could no longer be regarded as inherently evil when it was the essential ingredient that kept the mission alive. This became the foundation for one of Stephen's most important yet simple teachings, "Work is the material expression of love. Money is the material expression of work."

The Caravan was the staging ground for The Farm community. This period was the time when those on board began to recognize that they were not mere passengers, but crew on a sailing ship. As the captain, Stephen called the shots; he set the standards for others to follow. For example, he established that, rather than the buses leaving haphazardly as people would wake up, they would all drive off together. This meant that everyone needed to get up and moving at the same time, and so a drivers' meeting was held before every departure.

Stephen began each morning by going down the line of buses with a hammer, tapping on the bumpers as the resident alarm clock. It didn't take long before someone else stepped into this role, freeing Stephen for other responsibilities. Others took on the tasks of organizing work crews and acquiring food and basic medical care.

The need for competent medical care was taken to an entirely new level as women on The Caravan, pregnant when the group departed from San Francisco, began to give birth. Although the first few deliveries were rosy, beautiful experiences expressing the miracle of life, one baby didn't start breathing on its own and had to be coaxed and worked on. That was a wake-up call about the level of responsibility that was in store. Ina May, Stephen's wife, lost her baby when it was born prematurely on The Caravan. In her grief, Ina May vowed to become a midwife, dedicating her life to the health and safety of mothers and babies everywhere.

The Caravan went across the Northwest, through Minnesota, and all the way east to New York City. It dropped down to Washington, DC, and then through the South, stopping in places such as Nashville and Little Rock. The Caravan had grown in number, both in terms of people and vehicles, attracting new participants as the buses rolled through towns and cities. A modern Pied Piper, Stephen and his Caravan gave the hippie idealists a direction to follow.

The line of buses would stretch for miles.

One person who jumped on board when The Caravan passed through his college town described the decision to join this way: "These folks had been on the road for a number of months. I ran into people who were hippies just like me, very idealistic, trying to live in a way that aspired to higher ideals, cooperation, love, and respect for life . . . and more than respect for life, trying to live in a way where even anger was questioned. Here were some folks who were trying to be really conscious of their fragility as human beings, trying to work these things out. I was very attracted to this."

After about a year on the road, the long line of buses pulled back into San Francisco. The Caravan was over. But what now? Where do you park sixty, seventy buses for the last stop? Would everyone simply go back to looking for a place to crash, an apartment to rent, finding a job, returning to a scene that was now a shadow of its heyday?

Stephen described the experience of returning to San Francisco: "When we got back to the city, it had gone bad decadent. There were speed freaks sleeping in the doorways, skinny guys in black coats from New York selling heroin. It was awful! It was obvious that the nest had been fouled too much to build a fresh thing in."

Almost immediately, a meeting was called for the following Sunday at sunrise in Golden Gate Park. It was one thing to talk about the ideals of a new society based on spiritual values. Now it was time to put those ideals into practice. This could only be possible with land.

"We were only there a week," Stephen explained. The word went out, "Gather up The Caravan for a drivers' meeting on Sunday. We're pulling out." The drivers assembled one last time in San Francisco and said good-bye to the West Coast.

There had been numerous communes scattered about California. Several of the larger ones had already come into conflict with local authorities, who had sent out bulldozers to level the sprawl of hippie shacks in violation of virtually all local building codes. Land in California was also expensive. Then there was the issue of water—or lack of it. Water has always been a precious commodity in California, where rainfall is erratic and water is frequently piped in from vast distances to meet the demands of the state's cities and agriculture. It would be difficult to follow the ideal of becoming self-sufficient without enough water.

There was one other issue that came to bear. Stephen and, for lack of a better term, his followers, recognized that a primary goal was to instigate social change. They wanted to influence society by being a living example for others to use as a model. The media had successfully pigeonholed the young people in California as spaced-out flower children who could be written off as the crazy hippies. Anything coming from the West Coast could be dismissed in a similar fashion. Therefore, it was decided that the search for land would take place elsewhere, where the realms of possibility would be more open.

Word spread quickly. The excitement was almost palpable as it became clear the group would put its principles into practice. With the acquisition of land, this commitment to change would move beyond rhetoric to a new reality. No one knew where they were going, but in their hearts, this band of more than three hundred idealists knew the real journey was just beginning.

THREE

Looking for Land

Finding land was no small endeavor. The search was a series of false starts and important lessons. Some may say that it took divine intervention for so many pieces to have fallen into place. But followers of Stephen's teachings would say that it was the result of good karma, cause and effect, and that finding the right location for The Farm was the logical outcome of setting a pure intention.

The Search Begins

As The Caravan left San Francisco for the last time, it soon became clear that the road ahead would be full of challenges. Pulling into a rest stop before the buses had even left California, a cop came up and told the group they couldn't stay there and that they should keep moving. A few hours later, when The Caravan hit the state line, fifty cop cars were lying in wait with their red lights flashing. As it turned out, however, the police were not a problem. They were happy to see the group go and made themselves available to see that The Caravan did just that. The pattern of a police escort across state lines replayed over and over again as the convoy worked its way across the country. At each state line the cops on one side would pass The Caravan over to their counterparts on the other side and say, "These guys are okay."

As The Caravan continued eastward, the question of where to buy land and settle grew more meaningful. The intent was to get land on which to build a new way for people to live, but where was this ideal place? The obvious answer was to follow the vibes.

The Caravan had received a warm reception in Minneapolis. However, that was the only thing warm about the place. The harsh winters and limited growing season quickly eliminated any states that far north from the field of choices.

Fairly early on, it was decided that the South was the best place to begin looking for land. Of course, many people had reservations about whether West Coast hippies and the redneck portion of the country, so vividly depicted in the movie *Easy Rider,* were compatible.

Nashville, Tennessee, had made an impression on many of those who'd been on the previous road trip with Stephen. There, local residents had come out to visit and meet the hippies camped with The Caravan. In Nashville they encountered a genuine curiosity, along with friendly Southern hospitality. Farm folks eventually came to know this generous spirit as "down home"—the easygoing, slower pace that Southerners typically embrace. And it was a way of living that appealed to members of The Caravan. Nashville, therefore, became the new destination.

By the time The Caravan made it to Nashville, its journey had long been a subject in the press. The Caravan had even made the national evening news. Almost as if they were alerting the country to an impending storm, journalists, including respected CBS news anchor Walter Cronkite, called out the alarm, with the underlying message: "The hippies are coming! The hippies are coming! Why? They are going to buy land. They are going to buy land next to you!"

Arriving in Nashville, The Caravan was escorted to a newly opened campground facility on a man-made body of water called Old Hickory Lake. The camping areas were nestled among a large grove of oak trees, which provided shade from the intense summer sun. The high ridgetop gave views of the water, and it was a short stroll down to the lake, perfect for midnight swims under the Tennessee moonlight.

Shysters and Charlatans

Once the group had settled in, teams were dispatched to visit real estate offices and check local papers. Their mandate was to follow any lead north to Kentucky, as far west as Arkansas, and as far south as Mississippi or Alabama. These scouts were instructed to look for properties that had open, flat land for farming, trees for firewood and construction, creeks and springs to provide water, and enough acreage to allow the community to grow. It soon became apparent that the search required a cautious approach; nothing could be accepted at face value.

Stephen described one such encounter: "We went to look at some land up in Knob Lick, Kentucky. After we'd been there for a while, we came to realize that what was really going on was a family feud about whose land it was. We were merely a pawn in the feud." Nothing good could come from such an unwelcome beginning.

Back in Tennessee, a beautiful five-hundred-acre property outside of Nashville was seriously considered. Closer inspection, along with measurements and mathematical calculations, revealed that the place was really only about one hundred acres. It was time to back up trust with vigilance. There, in the midst of the Bible Belt, Stephen pointed out that the biblical verse "be wise as serpents, harmless as doves" had a new relevance.

The Caravaners had been camping at the park by Old Hickory Lake for nearly a month, and still there were no solid deals on the table. It was important that the group not overstay its welcome. No one wanted to risk losing the friendly atmosphere in Nashville. Then, a door opened by chance, a true stroke of luck.

"We decided, as big as we are, we need a voice. We should have a band," said Stephen. The idea was to put together an album and then go out on the road, using the band to draw an audience to hear Stephen speak about the new community, and about the nature of spiritual consciousness. One of the musicians chosen for the band had gone into downtown Nashville to trade in his acoustic twelve-string for a solid-body electric guitar suitable for rock-and-roll.

As the group discussed ideas on how best to get the word out about the new community, Stephen and the various musicians came up with the idea of forming a rock-and-roll band.

While in Gruhn Guitars, this Caravan musician struck up a conversation with a young woman who worked there. Like many young people of the time, she was fascinated by what the group was attempting to pull off. She let it be known that her parents owned an abandoned farm in Lewis County, about seventy miles south of Nashville. No one had lived on the land in over thirty-five years. She suggested that The Caravan could park the buses and live there while continuing to look for land.

Most of the 650-acre Martin farm was in forest; about thirty acres in the center had been cleared, where a house once stood. After a few phone calls and a meeting with the owner, permission was granted to stay on the land. To ease their introduction to rural Tennessee, the property owner passed on instructions to deliver a fifth of bourbon to Homer Sanders, the local caretaker of the land. The Caravan fired up all the engines and headed out.

The move took local reporters by surprise. Many had been following the exodus, keeping an eye on The Caravan and covering the unfolding story. This regular coverage had drummed up curiosity, and plenty of everyday Americans wanted to see where the buses would head next. Word spread quickly in the Nashville area that the buses were on the move, and people lined the small-town streets to watch the procession. It traveled south through Franklin and then Columbia, veering southwest through Mount Pleasant, and then turning west again toward Hohenwald and into Summertown, an unincorporated community. Not too far out of Summertown, the buses took a right turn off the pavement onto Drake Lane, a dusty dirt road, and came to a stop about a mile in, at the head of a trail that disappeared off into the woods.

Right away, there was a problem. The drive into the Martin farm was an old logging road, a rutted passage that ran along a fence line separating the land from the neighboring Smith property. The Martins and Smiths shared an easement on the logging road, which meant that it was jointly owned. Smith made it clear there was no way he would let this ragtag bunch of hippies use his road.

Some people in The Caravan became irate, reasoning that Smith had no right to block their way. Stephen remembers: "This made some of our folks mad. They felt, and rightly so, that we had a right to use the road, permission from the owners." More than a few Caravaners spoke up to say it was time to just start driving the buses in, whether Smith liked it or not.

Here was a moment when Stephen's greater maturity and his wisdom as a leader (or as he preferred to say, a teacher) came into play. His behavior at this juncture set the tone for things to come. There was no point in making an entrance that might anger a neighbor. The Caravan's first interaction with the local folks on the lane should be peaceful.

Meanwhile, all the buses were parked out along the edge of the road. There, someone noticed the remnants of another old logging road at a far corner of the property. Although the old road had grown up in saplings, some now as big as ten feet tall and a few inches in diameter, closer inspection revealed that this was indeed a route to the center of the property. It was another way in.

Most buses were equipped with small bow saws for cutting up sticks to feed the miniature woodstoves used to heat the rolling homes. With a clear mission and saws at the ready, little by little, the energetic young hippies opened up the old road. After many hours, the first buses wound their way down the quarter-mile path and found themselves in a large, open field in the middle of the property.

The soft, untrammeled earth in that central meadow had its drawbacks: a number of buses became stuck. But, as always, there was a way out of the problem. The potential of "monkey power" came to light, as a couple dozen people put their shoulders behind the sunken rear tires to keep each bus moving until it could be situated in a proper parking spot. By nightfall, every one of the buses had made it in. The Caravan had landed.

Homer Sanders

Homer Sanders was an early mentor of The Farm.

As caretaker, Homer Sanders's job was to watch over the land and ward off trespassers and log poachers. Homer lived with his wife and son in a small house just down and a bit off Drake Lane. He was a well-established character along the lane, with a reputation as someone not to be messed with. He had, at times, worked as a logger and run a saw mill. He'd been a bootlegger and a farmer. And like most country folk, he was a jack of all trades. Sometime before The Caravan arrived, Homer had been diagnosed with oral cancer and lost half his tongue, no doubt related to years of smoking and chewing tobacco. The result was that his Southern drawl was particularly difficult to understand.

Since he had no phone, the arrival of the hippies had taken Homer by surprise. But word made its way to him about the goings-on over at the Martin farm, and he loaded his shotgun, climbed on a mule, and headed over, bound and determined to run off these no-good freeloaders as quick as they had come.

Expecting the worst as he rode onto the property, Homer was taken aback by the scores of bright-eyed young people. The hippie women in their long dresses, even the men with their long hair, projected a gentle innocence, and their friendly faces made it hard for him to follow through on his intentions. Greeted with smiles, Homer found himself smitten with the boundless energy emanating from more than three hundred flower children who had made their way into his world.

When Homer met Stephen, he was surprised by his stature and presence and by the fact that Stephen treated him with respect, something not that common for a toothless hillbilly. A strong bond emerged between the two men, and Homer became The Farm's most important unofficial ambassador throughout the local area. He spread the word among the rest of the neighbors that the hippies were okay . . . and he would let them stay.

Homer took this role to heart. He went around town, to the local bank and stores and post office, and let everyone know the group was there with his approval. If Homer heard someone bad-mouthing the hippies, he would set them straight. Homer's early support was an important breakthrough that smoothed the way for The Farm to gain acceptance in the redneck South.

Over the ensuing years, Homer and The Farm community developed a close relationship. He reopened his sawmill and developed a business partnership with The Farm. In the process, he taught the young men of the community how to drop large trees, run heavy equipment, and produce lumber.

Homer also became something of a minor celebrity. News crews from all the local and national networks took their turn visiting The Farm, and Homer was often interviewed as well, describing how the Tennesseans had taken to their new hippie neighbors.

The Bust

The whole experiment almost came to an end before it got started, when local authorities discovered a large patch of marijuana planted by a few members of the group.

Stephen was adamant: "I was against planting pot. I was not a city guy. I knew this was not wilderness."

Much to their embarrassment, it turned out that the people tending the pot plants had placed the weed in plain sight, along trails frequented by local hunters. As Stephen tells the story, "Railroad guys were telling people, 'As you go through, look to your right. You've got a good chance you're going to see a naked hippie lady playing flute to a pot plant!'"

The bust brought widespread notoriety to The Farm when CBS reported it on the national evening news. The television piece opened from the desk of the news commentator, with a map of Tennessee over his shoulder and a star pinpointing the location of The Farm. "Earlier this summer we reported to you on a traveling commune of more than two hundred people who spent several weeks looking for a place to live. They had settled on a place near Nashville, but it didn't quite work out."

Cut to a throng of hippies and giggling hippie children walking alongside a cornfield. The narrator continues, "They say the group is held together by a kind of religion. They traveled over fifty thousand miles around the country looking for their own utopia, a farm, land to live on and to grow organic crops." Next the camera shows several squad cars driving through a gate onto the property. "But they found out the hard way that authorities don't consider every crop to fall into the organic vegetable category. One of them is hemp, marijuana, and state narcotics agents found over five hundred healthy plants. It was growing heartily alongside other crops on the Summertown, Tennessee, farm. Officials estimate that once processed, the crop would have been worth over $20,000. No one would own up to planting the marijuana, so authorities took four of the group's leaders into custody who were later released on bond. Stephen Gaskin, founder of the Monday Night Group, as they are called, says he knew nothing about the grass."

Next, a reporter at the scene interviews Stephen: "Stephen, are you growing marijuana here?" Stephen's reply, "Who me?" elicits a hearty chuckle from the crowd of hippies surrounding him. The reporter clarifies: "What are you growing here?" Stephen rattles off "corn, okra, tomatoes, carrots, peas." The reporter interjects, "Have you ever considered growing marijuana?" With his usual humor, Stephen replies, "Everybody always considers it." Again, his followers are amused.

Because of The Caravan, Stephen and the group had already received a lot of media attention and had experienced numerous encounters with police. No harm had come of this before and so no one understood the gravity of this situation.

Stephen and three other members of the group were charged with growing pot, found guilty, and sentenced to one to three years in state prison. The community had two lawyers as well as paralegals among its members and they devised an appeal strategy based on legal technicalities. But Stephen opted for the high road, choosing instead to pursue a defense based on the use of marijuana as a religious sacrament by The Farm Church. The case seemed like the perfect opportunity to focus national attention on the injustice of marijuana prohibition.

As the case was routed through the courts, each judge it came before viewed the issue as a hot potato and passed it on to a higher authority. After several years, the case reached the halls of the US Supreme Court, where it was refused and was returned to where it originated, and to the original judge.

By this time, Stephen and Judge Humphries, who had presided over the case in the local court, had become good friends. The judge had never had a case overturned and he was about to retire. Rather than sully Judge Humphries's record, Stephen made the decision to accept the penalty and do the time. Of course the other three defendants were forced to go along with him.

For the most part, Stephen and his three companions were well treated and even warmly received by the other inmates. The Farm's bands (at this point there were two rock-and-roll ensembles in the community) put on performances inside the prison and at other state detention facilities. Before the first year was up, Stephen and the other guys had been moved to a minimum security facility and were allowed out on work release. Stephen was able to visit The Farm on weekends to perform his Sunday Service. Just as they'd completed a year in prison, all four were set free.

Not long after the release of Stephen and the other three, Judge Humphries met with Stephen and Ina May at the courthouse to perform an official marriage ceremony. The judge also happened to be a singer, and in the years to follow, he brought his gospel group to perform several times at The Farm.

The Black Swan Ranch

In spite of the bust, the search for a more permanent home continued, and it may have even taken on a sense of urgency as it became clear the group needed to be settled down lest things begin to unravel. Quite fortunately, the solution to this problem was right around the corner.

If only it had been so easy to recognize. As group members sought a property to purchase, unbeknownst to them, the FBI had other ideas. And this made efforts to settle down that much more difficult. Requests through the Freedom of Information Act have revealed that Stephen and The Farm had been monitored by the FBI from the very beginning. Although most of the information in the reports has been blacked out, legend has it that the Tennessee office of the FBI was ordered to visit all the realty agents in the area with clear orders from their superiors: Do not sell the hippies any land. If they are unable to buy land, they will have to keep moving, and eventually the group will dissipate and disappear. Problem solved.

Not everyone received that message, though. Just a little way down the road from the Martin farm, Carlos Smith owned one thousand acres affectionately known as the Black Swan Ranch, named for Big Swan Creek that flowed nearby. About two hundred acres had been cleared and were being used as cattle pasture. Another one hundred acres or more had been logged recently and was starting to become overgrown with scrub shrubbery, red sumac mixed with blackberries and blackjack oak. The remaining acreage was in a majestic stand of southern hardwood forest, spread out over narrow fingers of ridgeline divided by steep valleys. A small creek bisected the land and numerous springs popped out from the hillsides.

Carlos and his family lived in a small ranch-style house near the property's edge, close to the road. There was a barn near the house, and a small shed was situated farther down a dirt road that ran through a cleared pasture. Like so many people of the time, Carlos was ready to be done with farming. This seemed like a good opportunity to sell and move on to something else. A deal was struck: one thousand acres for seventy dollars an acre. "An acre of land for less than the price of a kilo of grass," Stephen was fond of saying, with a wry chuckle.

The land purchase is one of the best illustrations of the commitment to the cause that was burning inside the hearts and souls of this core group of people who had dedicated themselves to the creation of this new community. Most of the money to pay for the property came from a few folks with small inheritances. Others who had accumulated a bit of savings contributed, too. Altogether, it was enough to pay for the thousand-acre tract in cash . . . and just like that, the hippies had their land.

It is important to note that Carlos didn't take the money and move away. He bought a house right in the middle of Summertown, just a couple of miles down the road from his farm. In essence he was making a statement to all the Tennesseans for miles around: "The hippies are good people. I think they will be good neighbors for our community." We always respected him for that.

The Black Swan Ranch property featured a long dirt road leading from the house for about three-quarters of a mile to the end of the cleared fields. There, a staging area had been established for earlier logging operations. From that point logging roads went down a series of ridges in several directions, almost like the fingers of a hand. The staging area was christened "Head of the Roads," and from there the rough and rutted logging roads were numbered and named in sequence: First Road, Second Road, Third Road, Fourth Road, and Fifth Road. In August 1971, the buses made their way down each one, pulling off to park along any place that appeared to be relatively flat.

Beyond The Farm's borders, in virtually all directions, lay thousands of acres of hardwood forest. At a thousand acres, The Farm was arguably already the largest hippie commune in the world, but land so cheap was an irresistible opportunity, so in 1973 a deal was struck to purchase the adjoining property. That gave the community another 750 acres. About one hundred acres of this land was cleared and ready for cultivation, including a "back forty," a plot known as Shoemaker Field. The rest was in forest. The Farm was now in possession of over three square miles.

The Smith family's 1950s-style ranch home became known as "The House," and it was the only residential building on the property. The House was turned into the main base of operations primarily because it had the only electricity, running water, bathroom, and phone line. One former bedroom sometimes functioned as a clinic, another as an office. The living room and front porch became Stephen's point of interface with the rest of the community. One might compare it to a guru giving "darshan" or a king holding court. Members of the community, Stephen's "students," would come there seeking his opinion, advice, or blessing. Crew leaders and managers in positions of responsibility gave reports. New arrivals wishing to join the community were required to make a personal connection with Stephen and make an agreement to accept him as their spiritual teacher, asking permission to stay. All of this made The House a focal point of Farm energy.

The groundwork for The Farm's economic organization had its beginnings back on The Caravan. To keep all the buses running, those who had money pitched in to buy gasoline. When The Caravan arrived at a new destination, people would hit the streets looking for work, again pooling the money earned to purchase food and gas for the entire group. Now that The Caravan had settled on the land, it was necessary to have a more formal, organized agreement about how the community would support itself—and everyone in it.

Anyone joining The Farm was expected to turn in all money and large possessions, such as a vehicle, but was allowed to keep personal items, such as a musical instrument. Because The Farm aimed to establish universal equality, everything was purchased collectively, from food to medicine to basic necessities, such as shampoo, soap, and toothpaste. All work was also shared, which included services performed inside the community and work done outside that generated income.

Any money that was earned was turned over to a central "bank" to be managed and distributed by a "bank lady," whose function was to give money to anyone who needed it, under a system that was loosely based on the book of Acts from the Bible. Acts 2:45 states: "And sold their possessions and goods, and parted them to all men, as every man had need."

This single aspect of Farm ethics would become an integral part of the community's identity and would set the tone for every aspect of life on The Farm to come.

FOUR

Three Days or the Rest of Your Life

The 1970s saw a cultural shift away from farm life in America. When Stephen and his followers landed in Summertown, Tennessee, in the summer of 1971, young people who had been born and raised in the rural areas of the country were leaving the family farms to find work in the city. The Farm's neighbors, who represented perhaps the last generation of their kind, were thrilled to see a group of young people leaving the cities and earnestly seeking their knowledge of farming. Many of these neighbors took the hippies of The Farm under their wings, becoming teachers and mentors.

In retrospect, the mid-1970s were in many ways the peak period of hippie culture. Thanks in part to the mass media, the ideals of the counterculture were broadcast across the nation. Baby boomers were in their twenties and early thirties, still young enough not to have put down roots. Millions of boomers hit the road in search of something, even if they were not quite sure what they were seeking. The Farm became a mecca and for many a required stop on their journey. Up to ten thousand people a year would come by for a visit to see for themselves this most visible example of the counterculture alternative to the capitalist status quo.

Attracting New Folks

For many young people, The Farm was an alternative to college. Often those attracted to it were university dropouts, individuals who could not see the relevance of pursuing higher education and a career path leading to the corporate world. The pool of people arriving at The Farm tended to be highly educated, which fostered a forum for discussions on philosophy, world affairs, existential literature, and humanity's relationship to the universe. It was a stimulating environment that gave those making a commitment to stay the feeling that they were active participants in the creation of a new structure for society. They were fashioning a reality from the Aquarian vision—the Sixties' ethos of a boundary-breaking, uninhibited, revolutionary take on life.

In the spring of 1973, Stephen went out on the road with The Farm Band, traveling to cities all across the country. After playing music for about an hour, the band would take a break and Stephen would talk about The Farm, displaying a slide show to illustrate what was taking place in the backwoods of Tennessee. Our hometown of Louisville, Kentucky, was the first stop on that first tour.

I will never forget seeing Stephen and the band at that concert. Deborah and I had learned about The Farm just about a year before while reading an article in *Mother Earth News*, a brand-new magazine about homesteading. There was a full page of pictures describing life on The Farm, and we weren't overly impressed. Everyone looked very serious. Still, when we heard that Stephen and the band were coming to town, we decided to check them out. Although we were not necessarily searching for a spiritual guide, like many of our generation, we were seeking a greater understanding of the meaning of life. We had been to see a couple of other spiritual teachers who had come from or were influenced by the culture of India, and each fit our impression of what "spiritual" was supposed to be. This, however, was quite different.

The band rocked hard. Then, when Stephen began to talk, he told the audience that our town was not very hip, that it had been dumbed down by the dominance of the tobacco and whiskey industries. I understood where he was coming from and grew more interested.

Next, he started getting on this guy's case, an audience member who was wearing a Rolling Stones T-shirt with that well-known logo: big lips and a tongue sticking out. Stephen confronted him: "If you're wearing a Mick Jagger T-shirt, and you buy all Mick Jagger's albums, and you go to his concerts, and you think Mick Jagger is really cool, then Mick Jagger is your spiritual teacher. You have to question if he is really worthy of so much of your attention. I mean, what is he really saying or doing?"

This impressed me, because I had been reluctant to follow the guidance of a so-called spiritual teacher. But Stephen's reasoning gave me a new perspective, and as we watched the slide show about life on The Farm, I began to weigh the significance of Stephen's words. Here was a community of fellow hippies working together for a common purpose. It was incredible. Deborah and I immediately made plans to see The Farm for ourselves.

We were both nineteen and had already been married for two years. I had graduated high school a year early, and Deborah had left school before entering her senior year. To our parents' dismay, we had no interest in college. Our general plan was to buy some land where we could grow our own food and live close to nature. We also felt a responsibility to continue working as political activists and were drawn to get involved in the current movement for cultural change, to do what we could to bring about a more just society in a world that seemed headed toward calamity. The Farm clicked with us on so many levels: the members championed getting back to the land, were socially and politically active, and followed a vegetarian diet. Of special importance to Deborah, The Farm promoted natural childbirth and midwifery. The Farm seemed to be the perfect fit for us.

On our way down to Summertown, we picked up a couple of hitchhikers just outside of Nashville, and it turned out they were also headed to The Farm. We pulled into The Farm entrance and were instructed to park, and then to sit with a large group gathered under the shade of a tree. I think we were taken aback when we observed Farm members passing around a can of 7-Up. White sugar? Junk food? What's up with that? The people in charge seemed to be focused on one fellow in particular, and he didn't appear to be very happy about it. It had something to do with how he was treating his girlfriend or wife.

After about an hour, we were sent down to stay with a couple living in a school bus. They did not hold back and openly challenged what we intended to do with the rest of our lives. It made us question our direction and goals, and it became clear to us that the ethics here dovetailed with ours. This community, we felt, embodied a vision for the future that we hoped would change the world. We knew this was what we wanted to do. A month later, Deborah and I came back to ask Stephen if we could join The Farm, and after a few days we caught up with him driving down the road. He stopped to talk to us and we made our request. Stephen said, "Well, have you got all your stuff with you?" We had not presumed it would be possible to move there without asking first, and answered no. "Find me when you get back," he said and drove away. Deborah and I went back home, tied up loose ends, gathered up our stuff, and moved to The Farm in late summer, ready to live in our VW van.

After we had been living on The Farm for several months, one of our friends brought up the fact that we had never actually made our agreement with Stephen. Deborah and I went up to Stephen after the next Sunday Service in the meadow. At first no one said anything; we just looked at each other and "vibed." Finally I mumbled something like, "I guess we're living here now." We were all smiling, then we hugged, and that was it. Nothing more needed to be said. The connection was telepathic.

Besides the concerts, another step The Farm took that attracted hundreds of new members was the publication of its first book, *Hey Beatnik!*. This title was a tongue-in-cheek rejection of the hippie label used by the press to marginalize the ideas of the counterculture. But the book itself was meant to shine a light on The Farm lifestyle, its success, and its spiritual values.

Hey Beatnik! provided the perfect overview of virtually every aspect of Farm life, including growing our own food, managing our medical needs, raising our kids, getting along with our neighbors, and much more. Sprinkled throughout were essays by Stephen on the nature of a spiritual path and the moral values that established the framework that held the community together. The book sold well and became a popular manual, laying out a blueprint that could be used by anyone wanting to start an intentional community.

The volume of visitors arriving on a daily basis required The Farm to become organized lest it be overrun. Having experienced the shortcomings of crash pads and the "anything goes" anarchy of San Francisco and the West Coast, Stephen recognized that The Farm's survival depended on establishing boundaries as well as a way to efficiently integrate newcomers.

The Gate

The Gate was the first stop for anyone and everyone who came to The Farm. It could be said that without The Gate, The Farm would not have survived. This was the portal through which all passed, and its keepers maintained a firm handle on who was coming in and how long they were allowed to stay. Their function, also, was to determine which people were serious and viable candidates for membership. The rest would be sent on their way.

It wasn't uncommon for visitors arriving at The Gate to show up anxious, even a bit pushy, a common symptom of life on the road. They were often shocked when asked to slow down and sit a spell, sometimes for up to several hours, before being allowed to enter The Farm. The people working The Gate became expert at spotting new arrivals who had bad vibes, something to hide, criminal intent, or simply a bit of a temper. This didn't necessarily mean such a person couldn't come in for a visit. It was The Gate Crew's job to poke around a bit and find out what was below the surface. Could this person relax and let go or was this someone determined to cling to an uptight attitude? The Gate Crew found that when people were faced with the truth about themselves in a way that allowed them space to change, they would usually adjust their attitudes and the process could move forward.

Everyone took a turn working at The Gate, screening new arrivals to determine which ones were truly interested in joining the community.

Of course most folks who came through were like us: sweet, young hippie types seeking to make a better world, whether it was on The Farm or in some other way they'd yet to find. For many, The Farm was a way station on their personal journey, and it offered an opportunity to see that there were alternatives to joining the suburban rat race.

At The Gate, visitors made a verbal agreement about how long they would stay: one, two, or three days. Then they would be sent down on The Farm. For the first several years, single people would be sent to a single men's or women's tent, and couples would be placed with a family.

As the number of visitors grew from hundreds to thousands of people a year, the community built a large Visitors' Tent, capable of housing and feeding thirty to forty people at a time. Couples in the community would take turns living in the Visitors Tent for a week or two, integrating the flow of newcomers. They worked closely with the folks at The Gate, monitoring the situation, sending most people back out the door when their time was up, but also helping those who wanted to stay take the next steps to become part of the community.

Stephen came up with the catch phrase "Three days or the rest of your life." Visitors to The Farm were allowed to stay for up to three days. During that time they would be assigned to a work crew, share meals, and get an up-close and personal view of Farm life. After three days they had to make a choice: they could leave or request an extended stay in hopes of becoming a permanent member.

"The rest of your life" defined the commitment that was expected, and in truth required, for The Farm to be a strong and cohesive community. The Farm would not last if it was only a short-term home to people passing through. The community had been around long enough for its members to realize that the stakes were high and that anything less than a sincere commitment sold short those who were giving it their all.

Deborah and I took several turns working the Visitors' Tent, and it was something we really enjoyed. It gave us a break from our regular jobs, and it provided more time for me to spend with our two kids and for us to be together as a family. There was an intense energy in the Visitors' Tent that I liked. Here we were at the crossroads, with people passing through who were curious and full of questions. One fellow, a doctor just out of medical school, ended up staying and became one of my lifelong friends. Decisions people made in the Visitors' Tent could forever change their lives.

Of the thousands who visited The Farm each year, between one hundred and two hundred people would stay and give it a go. After about five years, the population had grown from the original three hundred Caravaners to a bustling one thousand members.

Although most of the buses and tents where we lived were outfitted with some type of small kitchen, for the first several years it was deemed more efficient to have a central kitchen prepare meals for everyone in the community three times a day. Each meal had a different crew of cooks. In our first months on The Farm, Deborah and I took on a breakfast shift, arriving at three or four in the morning to be ready for the work crews heading out into the fields or getting started with other tasks.

In summer months we usually had plenty of vegetables, but it was a different story in the winter, when The Farm's fields were fallow and little money was coming in from outside work. Winter meals could be very bleak. The second year was especially hard and came to be known as Wheat Berry Winter, because wheat berries were often the only thing on the menu. These kernels of grain were served up like brown rice, but they are much tougher to chew and digest.

Lunchtime could be especially chaotic and was almost humorous in its degree of inefficiency. It could take up to three hours to get through the extremely long lines. No one seemed to mind, as it was just another time to socialize and get to know each other.

Over the course of several years, the community developed multiple kitchens in different locations to decentralize the task of serving breakfast and lunch to work crews. Eventually evening meals were prepared and served primarily at home, which coincided with the shift from people residing in single-family buses to the multifamily communal living arrangements that ultimately provided housing for most of The Farm's members.

Building Our Town

As the population exploded, the community needed to make changes to accommodate the influx of new members and to make life on The Farm more efficient. It had become apparent that this was more than a quaint commune and that the task at hand was to build a town from scratch.

There was no time to waste. The population was quickly growing beyond what could be handled by the community's infrastructure and housing. Buses were essentially single-family homes and that was a living arrangement now deemed inefficient because it wasted resources. After all, a good-sized woodstove could keep one family warm or it could keep thirty people warm using about the same amount of firewood.

Everyone knew that living in the buses was a stopgap and that the intent was to build permanent dwellings. One of the first home designs was called a "D-frame." It used trusses shaped like the letter *D*, and the gentle arch gave the buildings a barnlike appearance. The trusses were built out of locally harvested oak. We would create a dwelling by arranging eight or ten trusses in a row to form the walls and a roof. On the interior, a loft in the upper part of the arch served as a bedroom; the area below was divided into kitchen and living room space. Wings could be extended out from either side of the arch to create two additional rooms and even more living space. A number of D-frame homes were built before it was decided that even these were too expensive, mainly because they could only house one—or at most two—families at a time. The D-frames, as well as other small cabins that a few people built, could not address the housing needs of a population growing by one hundred to two hundred people every year.

In the search for something that could serve the community on a massive scale, we discovered that army surplus tents could be purchased for about twenty-five dollars apiece. Each 16-by-32-foot tent could house two or more couples or fifteen to twenty single folks. Tents began popping up everywhere like mushrooms in the forest. Even large public spaces, including The Farm Store and the canning and freezing operation, started out as army tents.

It was decided from the start that the tents needed to have wooden floors; no one should be living directly upon the ground. To get lumber and other building materials, a crew was assembled to travel to the nearby towns and the countryside in search of old barns, houses, and other types of buildings to dismantle. This turned out to be a service that many of our neighbors appreciated. Instead of paying someone for the demolition and site cleanup, they found that the hippies on The Farm would do all the work for free in exchange for the lumber, windows, doors, roofing tin, and other materials. As the word spread among our neighbors, The Farm's Wrecking Crew was in high demand. A core group of seven to ten guys formed the main crew, rallying as many as twenty to thirty extras when many hands were needed. An entire home could be brought to the ground and hauled away over the course of two to three days, and it would take another day or two for cleanup.

The Wrecking Crew became experts at demolition, salvaging a wide assortment of materials that were used for the construction of most of the community's homes and buildings.

One of the first big demolition jobs the crew took on was at an old tobacco warehouse in the town of Mount Pleasant, about ten miles down the road from The Farm. The warehouse had been constructed from massive, high-quality timbers, the likes of which do not exist anymore. This salvage was considered a major score. The crew also tore down several gymnasiums, which supplied many truckloads of tongue-and-groove hardwood flooring that was used in buildings throughout the community.

One of our most memorable demolition jobs occurred when The

Wrecking Crew took on a massive three-story former clothing factory in the center of downtown Pulaski, the town known as the birthplace of the Ku Klux Klan. It seemed to us an amazing turnaround to have a colorful array of hippies on display in the heart of the Deep South. I joined the crew just after the job started, and I was impressed that we could pull off something this big.

The building was owned by an adjacent bank that wanted to put a parking lot in its place. The old factory, constructed around the turn of the century, had thick walls of brick several layers deep. This demolition yielded many treasures. Literally tons of bricks were brought back to The Farm and used on the exterior of several of our larger public buildings. We got a lot of lumber, too. But some salvage was more useful as currency. Truckloads of copper wire from the building were hauled several hours south to Birmingham and sold for scrap metal, generating income to cover the expenses we incurred on the job. We sold some of the bricks and other salvaged materials, using the money to buy tools and heavy equipment, such as a dump truck. Although hauling heavy timber and the more dangerous tasks were performed by The Farm men, other jobs were performed by The Farm women. The mortar between the bricks had to be chipped away with a special hammer. Dozens of women were brought out to the job site to do this work.

When the job was completed, bank officials invited everyone who had worked on the project to a large banquet in our honor. It was a very sweet gesture, and we got a real taste of Southern hospitality. Clearly these jobs were very important to The Farm, as much for the goodwill they developed as for the building materials they generated.

A third large project that had a tremendous impact on the community was the demolition of a round-roof warehouse in the town of Columbia, just a block away from the courthouse and town square. This time the building to be torn down was owned by a church, and it was also to be replaced by a parking lot. I was twenty at the time, had been a crew member for less than a year, and had worked my way up to the position of number two man in charge. I worked up the proposal and shook hands on the deal, getting us $2,000 plus all the salvaged building materials.

Huge bow-shaped steel trusses about sixty feet wide formed the support system for this building's round roof. These were brought back to The Farm, but rather than simply rebuild with them to create a structure in the shape of the warehouse, Farm builders decided to ponder the design awhile. Perhaps they could come up with a more creative use for these unusual structural elements. After a few years, an idea hatched: We stood the trusses on end and joined them together at a center point to form a massive dome. Between the trusses, we constructed arches that we made of steel salvaged from a bunch of telephone switching centers that had been given to the community as scrap. The Meeting Hall dome was designed to hold one thousand people, and its location next to The Farm Store in the very center of the community made it a signature structure, our own Eiffel Tower.

Now, with a steady flow of materials coming in, building the town could begin in earnest. We undertook a complete upgrade of our dwelling units, turning the tents into comfortable—if still temporary—homes. Grade B lumber was used to build the structural support for the floor systems, wall framing, and tent roofs. Holes were cut into the canvas walls and salvaged windows were installed to let in more light. Real doors were framed in. Interior walls were built to divide the space and create bedrooms, offering a little privacy.

But the real goal was to build permanent homes. We had set aside the highest-quality materials for the construction of permanent buildings, and, one by one, large structures capable of housing thirty to forty people were being built up and down the roads of The Farm, all from salvaged and recycled materials. Most of The Farm's early buildings had roofs covered with salvaged tin, and some still do.

The salvage operation was a perfect fit for the early Farm. Community members were eager to lend their muscle to the hands-on work that demolition requires. We were a large pool of free labor, bringing in truckloads of lumber, block, steel, windows, and doors, all at virtually no cost to the community. The steady flow of what seemed to be an unlimited supply of construction materials made it possible to build the vast array of public buildings and dozens of homes that formed the foundation of The Farm's housing infrastructure.

Another form of salvage operation underscored The Farm's ability to take on oversized projects: house moving. In the nearby town of Columbia, plans were under way to build a dam that would flood a large valley. Before the homes there were to be submerged by rising waters, the buildings were offered to anyone who wanted to haul them away. Several members stepped up to learn how to move a home intact, and in this case, nearly forty miles from its original location to The Farm.

Special house jacks, capable of lifting up to ten tons, were used to gently lift a house off its foundation. By this method, a house was raised inch by inch until it was far enough off the ground that a semitrailer could be placed beneath its center. Windows and doors that might crack under the stress were removed before the trailer started down the road toward The Farm. The transport was carefully coordinated with local authorities to chart a route that would steer the truck and its house cargo away from narrow bridges and help it avoid stretches of highway with low-lying electrical or telephone lines.

The Farm's members learned the art and science of moving entire structures.

The moves always generated a lot of attention. They really were a spectacle. One of the salvaged houses was used for The Farm's Welcome Center, another as a home called "The Wide Load House." A large church was moved to the community that became The Farm Clinic.

Early on, while Stephen was away on a speaking tour, and when most of the community were still living in buses and tents, members thought they'd surprise Stephen and his family by building them a large home. They used oak timbers, and the finished house featured a large stone fireplace centered along one wall. Stephen appreciated the gesture but never really felt right about it. The home stood out from the forest, was visible from the main road, and in contrast to other Farm dwellings, appeared to be a mansion. Stephen and his family lived in it for about a year, but then said they felt that living there put them on a pedestal. It wasn't right for them to live in such a nice place while most folks were still in buses and an array of other structures. Stephen chose instead to have a tent home built for his family and him to the same standards as the others on The Farm. This home was situated on a ridge away from the rest of The Farm's population so that Stephen would not be readily available to the constant stream of community members seeking his counsel. As the community's spiritual guide, Stephen could easily spend all his waking hours in consultation with people over petty matters.

Early Communications

When The Caravan first arrived on the land, the buses spread out in all directions, across hundreds of acres. Basic communication traveled by word of mouth, slow and unreliable at best. To signal the start of each workday and to awaken everyone for the Sunday morning service, a handful of people located at intervals across The Farm would blow into conch shells, natural trumpets whose warm tones resonated with the community members.

To give you an idea of how rural the area was at the time, consider that the more than three hundred residents of The Farm were required to share their phone with six neighbors, an arrangement known as a "party line." Only one person could use the phone line at a time. If you picked up the receiver when the phone was in use, you could hear the conversation in progress. Waiting for your turn to place a call was a time-consuming process. On weekends and especially on Sunday afternoons, many people on The Farm would line up to place long-distance calls to their parents, the usual check-in that any kid or young adult might do on a regular basis. Since phone time was precious, a new job developed: phone operator. This person kept the running list of who was next in line to make a call and was also responsible for picking up the phone to find out if any neighbors were using the line. In between each call made by someone from The Farm, no calls were placed for about fifteen to twenty minutes to give the neighbors a chance to use the line. The simple task of making a call home could take three or four hours, mostly spent waiting on the porch until your turn came along.

As The Farm Midwives began to understand the weight of their role in the community, it became clear that a better method of communication was needed—something other than sending a runner on foot to find a midwife when a baby was on the way.

The community was fortunate to have a few people in its midst with a background in electronics. We managed to acquire a large quantity of scrapped or salvaged copper-coated steel phone wire and strung up a spaghetti network of lines through the trees, crisscrossing the forest. Initially the "Beatnik Bell" was much like an intercom or a party line with thirty to forty people sharing a single line. Standard telephone handsets were used to access the community-wide conversation, but instead of a ring, each location was assigned a Morse code tone. People trained their ears to monitor the beeps in the background, listening for the right code to know when the call was meant for them. Pregnant couples would have a line and a phone installed at their home a week or so before their baby was due so they could directly contact The Farm Midwives.

We kept this arrangement in operation for a couple of years before replacing it with a hand-me-down system donated by a local telephone company. A special building was constructed to house the multiple rows of eight-foot-high banks of relays and switches. This new internal phone service enabled The Farm to distribute dozens of individual phone numbers to our members. On top of that, a half dozen outside lines were routed to the building. A team of switchboard operators manned stations twenty-four hours a day, manually connecting callers on The Farm to the outside world, and vice versa. Mom and Dad could call The Farm and be connected directly to their hippie children and grandchildren.

All of the homes and businesses were connected to The Farm's internal phone system, dubbed "Beatnik Bell."

Wells and Water Towers

The original house on The Farm property had its own well, which supplied water to the kitchen and bathroom. In addition to the bathtub and shower, The House had the only flush toilet on The Farm, and it would remain the sole flusher on the land for many years.

The community's primary residential area was more than a mile from The House, so establishing a water source closer to the residents was an early priority. A spring was found on the side of a hill in a location that could serve most of The Farm's residents. We acquired a small, used water tower about thirty-five feet tall with a several-hundred-gallon tank and placed this at the top of the ridge above the spring. Then, two water spigots were installed for filling jugs: one at the foot of the tower, and another a quarter mile away, near The Farm Store, a central gathering place where food was distributed.

Since there was no electricity, a system was set up to run the water pump using Volkswagen engines. We had a ready supply of these motors pulled from the many VW buses and Beetles driven onto the property by the young hippies who regularly joined the community. Driving these vehicles around The Farm wasn't an option. The dusty dirt roads choked the VW air-cooled engines. But we put those engines to work pumping water, and whenever one blew up, we could easily replace it from our abundant inventory. The life of an engine running nonstop day after day was short, so a replacement was always kept on standby.

This modernization created a new job on The Farm. To keep the water tank filled, someone had to operate, monitor, and maintain the pump and engine, which had to run much of the day and into the night to keep up with demand. The gas tank needed to be kept topped off, the oil checked, and the whole operation required a hands-on guard who could troubleshoot problems as they arose. Guys took on four-hour shifts for this very important but generally boring and loud task. This went on for more than three years before electricity was finally supplied that far down into the community and we could replace the inefficient system by a pump with an automatic start and shutoff.

The source of a spring is often from the water table relatively close to the surface of the earth, and the water can easily become contaminated. Springs are also susceptible to droughts, and they are likely to go dry after long periods without rain. The solution, then, was to drill a well. As might be expected, we wanted to do this ourselves, so we bought an old drilling rig. Actually, it wasn't a drill at all but an old-fashioned impact rig that repeatedly slammed a weighted piece of steel, pounding it deeply into the ground. It took the drilling crew several months before they hit water at about fifty feet down, near The Farm Store. When it was decided a second well was needed, we called in a local well-drilling company. It took the professionals just three days to dig down about 150 feet, where they found a powerful aquifer.

The task was building a town from scratch with very little money but a tremendous amount of enthusiasm. Every day that we went out to work on The Farm, we could feel ourselves making a vital contribution to our community. It was exciting to know that our efforts helped move our vision for a new society forward. Ultimately, this work was all about the material plane, and one of Stephen's primary teachings was that all things emanate from the spiritual plane and are transferred to the material. If we focused our attention on the spiritual and put our house in order, everything on the material side would come together.

At The Farm we were putting our spiritual beliefs into action. To quote another of Stephen's proverbs, "Meditation is just another form of sitting on your ass." In other words, being spiritual wasn't about thinking holy thoughts, chanting, and walking about with goofy smiles of eternal bliss. It was about taking care of each other and learning how to live together in close quarters, constantly "up in each other's thing." It was about dealing with the subconscious, the invisible realm where personalities clash and conflicting egos bump heads. As it turned out, just learning to live together was the biggest challenge of all.

FIVE

Living Together

Because most members at this time were in their twenties and thirties, there was still plenty of incentive for an active social life—in other words, to party. For most of us, this essentially meant hanging out and laughing a lot, listening to or making music, and having a good time. In the outside world, circles of young people often have one friend who accepts the role of party house host and whose home becomes the weekend gathering spot. When the chemistry was right, every house on The Farm felt like a party house, with large groups of young people drawn together, celebrating life by living on the edge, in a way Mom and Dad just didn't understand. It was a blast.

The energy created by so many people living together and sharing a common spiritual purpose was undeniable . . . and a lot of fun!

Working It Out

This experiment in communal living on a mass scale came to define life on The Farm in the mid to late 1970s and early 1980s. Living in such close quarters meant that people got to know each other quickly, discovering the good as well as the bad, including those character flaws that

Stephen called our "egos." Because each person (supposedly) came to the community with the intention to grow spiritually, it was expected that those closest to you would inform you about your personal shortcomings. These typically included such habits as getting uptight; speaking harsh, unkind words; having a self-serving attitude; and displaying a number of other undesirable mannerisms.

"Working it out" was about being honest and open; it meant that we were obligated always to speak the truth to each other. If a person did or said something that made you feel uncomfortable, you were expected to address the issue. It was important to bring these issues forward so that hurt and resentment would not linger in the subconscious. When someone came forward to discuss this kind of a problem, in Farm jargon we'd say: "I have subconscious with you." Often just bringing things out in the open would be enough to relieve the tension and help everyone remain friends.

On the other hand, when offering your thoughts on how someone needed to change, there was no guarantee that they would be open to the information. That person was just as likely to become defensive, even argumentative. When, as was often the case, the dispute was between two people, each one had a role in the situation and both naturally had something to say to each other. These conversations became known as the "sort out," referring to the task of hearing out both sides to determine the truth. When it worked, it was a foundation for great personal growth.

Perhaps nowhere was this more evident and beneficial than in the changes that could take place within the relationship of a couple. On The Farm we observed that after the honeymoon period was over, it was not uncommon for spouses to begin taking each other for granted, falling into a pattern of bickering. Hurtful things could be said, gruff attitudes could become the norm, and a couple in a relationship might not treat each other as well as they would a friend or stranger. For couples living alone in a single-family home, these energy loops could continue to progress in a downward spiral until the relationship was beyond repair and ended in a separation.

Because couples on The Farm lived in communal households, their relationships played out before an audience that observed each person's role. These folks brought an outside yet intimate perspective and could call the two spouses on their "stuff" (behavior and habits). Since this period on The Farm was also in step with the women's movement, a cultural awakening in the United States during which traditional male and female roles were being challenged, frequently it was the husband who was the main focus of attention and put on the spot for the way he was treating his partner, such as being overbearing, intimidating, and disrespectful. Even though we were hippies, we could fall back into stereotypic gender roles we'd seen in the relationships of our elders. It all added up to the one thing every guy dreaded—being labeled an "MCP," or male chauvinist pig.

I credit The Farm with saving my marriage. As a young couple who had married just out of high school, we were not expected to make it. The odds were against us staying together. We had been living on The Farm less than a year when I found myself as the focal point of a "sort out." A circle of people got on my case, telling me that my surly behavior was demeaning to Deborah. I squirmed for a bit, but I had to "cop," or admit I was in the wrong, and that she deserved to be treated better. I was able to see that I was falling short of my own ideals, slipping into "square" social patterns that had been programmed into my psyche as an American male.

Of course this issue didn't get resolved with just one "sort out." As happens with any married couple, we would have our ups and downs, and it was always the valuable insight of friends who knew us both that helped us get through any tough times, allowing us to grow.

Experiments in Marriage

Living together helped everyone learn and gain a better understanding of the complexities and challenges in human relationships. This became abundantly clear as The Farm came to terms with a unique experiment that originated in the euphoric lovefest of San Francisco's Haight-Ashbury.

Inspired by psychedelic insights that revealed love as the key to the universe, a number of couples bonded into what became known as a "four-marriage." It entailed two married couples joining together to create a new "marriage" of four individuals. Those engaged in four-marriage, which began with Stephen's family and those couples closest to him, felt they were making a commitment to a new level of human relationship, interpreted to be a higher rung on the ladder of the spiritual path leading to enlightenment.

Many of the four-marriages survived the trip from San Francisco to Tennessee and formed the nucleus for a number of the first communal households. Now faced with the day-to-day realities of living together, the afterglow quickly began to fade. Hours upon hours of sorting out the complexities of being married to three other people made it readily apparent that this was an idea that had run its course. Several of the four-marriages held on for a few years, but eventually all the partners separated and returned to monogamous relationships. Some went back to their original mates, while others exchanged spouses. It can be said that we experience our greatest periods of growth during times of struggle. As proof of their growth, the individuals who went through this experience continued to serve as important leaders of the community and mentors in compassion and strength.

Communal Chemistry

The communal households were referred to as "group head," a description of the group mind and subsequent gestalt personality that was a reflection of the people who were all living together. Most people understand the concept of chemistry between two people, but this same energy was evident in communal living arrangements. When a group head had good chemistry, the people living within it enjoyed being together. It could just as easily go the other way, with constant friction, bickering, and an uptight scene.

People who worked or lived together were called a "Group Head."

One way to determine the mental health of a household was to look at how general tasks were performed. For instance, the way a house managed the everyday chore of doing the dishes told a lot about the group as a whole. Since there was no electricity, all dishes were washed by hand, and a household of twenty to forty people could generate a lot of dirty dishes. Ideally, everyone would simply pitch in together every night to do kitchen cleanup until all the work was done. However, you couldn't always count on everything to work out so smoothly. People who carried large responsibilities, such as The Midwives, might have erratic schedules. Large families with several children might feel they needed to take care of getting the kids to bed and so excuse themselves from kitchen duties. Or it could simply come down to the fact that some folks were go-getters who knew how to take care of business, whatever the task, and others were more laid back, or "low juice," oblivious to the needs of the home, self-absorbed, or "on their own trip." There was also the issue of standards. Some were not bothered by a dirty kitchen; others could not rest until cleanup had been completed.

Often the best solution for a household was to devise a schedule and assign tasks. With a schedule, all household members had a turn and knew what was expected of them, and sometimes they were free to do something else.

The House Meeting was where these types of problems were figured out and we talked about how to be better organized. These meetings also presented an opportune time to confront those who were not carrying their fair share of the load. Household tasks covered in these discussions ranged from getting firewood to making home improvements, and from child care to potential new housemates.

Just as unresolved issues might create subconscious resentment between two people, rifts could develop within a household, leading to a more broadscale, simmering anger. Sometimes bitterness in the group was directed toward a particular couple or divisions arose about topics such as different parenting and discipline styles. Ideally, compromises would be reached and good vibes would return, but just as often the solution was for someone to move out. Fortunately, another aspect of the early hippie communal lifestyle was that a family's entire worldly possessions could fit in the back of a pickup truck, making it possible to move with only a moment's notice.

Typically, living arrangements were in a state of constant flux. With each household functioning almost as an independent commune, Farm members were able to try many different living arrangements until the perfect combination of chemistry and personality was found. People might move because they wanted to live with new friends, upgrade their living conditions, or share a house where their children would have playmates of a similar age. Each move would set off a chain reaction, producing a series of other household changes as the population of The Farm shifted into a new configuration.

Ultimately we learned that wherever there are people, there will be problems. By taking the time to acknowledge and talk about these problems, we found that most issues could be resolved and friendships restored. Going one step further, we came to realize that it takes work to live in harmony, and we needed to hone our interpersonal skills every day to achieve that outcome. The more we put into our relationships, and the more open we were with our friends, the stronger our community would be. With work, we developed an atmosphere of cooperation and built deep and lasting friendships.

Communal Living

Households that didn't maintain cleanliness standards were susceptible to the dreaded scourge of crowded living conditions everywhere: roaches. To be fair, even tidy houses could suffer from a roach infestation, especially if someone moved from a house with roaches into one that had been roach-free. And people moved around a lot. Roaches can hide inside cardboard packing boxes, photo albums, books, anywhere there's a crevice. A roach can always find a place to stow away.

Calling an exterminator was out of the question. It would be too expensive; there were just too many houses to fumigate. Moreover, none of us wanted chemical poisons sprayed in our homes, especially with so many young kids around.

The solution? Freeze the critters out! At some point during the winter, when temperatures were dropping into the teens, a household would let its woodstove fire die out, move all of the furniture outside, drain the water pipes, open all the doors and windows, and then everyone would find someplace else to stay for three nights. It worked! In less than a week, the house could be rendered roach-free.

Child care was another part of everyday life that benefited from scheduling. Because Farm families were in their childbearing years, many of them had young children, and it was generally accepted that moms needed to be home with their kids, while dads went off to work. However, most women also were actively engaged in some type of job in the community. By sharing child care, mothers were able to spend time at home and go out to work. When the children got older, they went to The Farm School, and mothers could spend even more hours at work in the community.

In an effort to provide child care and encourage women's participation in The Farm workforce, some facilities set up day care on site. The canning and freezing operation had a space set up for the "kid herd," with multiple bunk beds for naps and a fenced play area. Moms could take turns processing food and watching kids. This arrangement worked well for new mothers, because they could be close at hand for feeding time or to attend to any other personal care their children might need.

Naturally, every household desired entertainment of some kind in the evenings. Because rock and roll was an essential part of our generation's culture, many of us played guitar, and most houses included a few musicians who could lead a sing-along or get people dancing.

In the early years, there were no TVs on The Farm, and as might be expected, the so-called "squawk boxes" were considered evil and were therefore taboo. Then The Farm was featured in a one-hour show about intentional communities, hosted by comedian Jonathan Winters. A TV was purchased and set up in The Farm Store so we could watch the show. Despite our bias against the medium, it was exciting to see The Farm depicted on screen.

At about this time, one of the big three broadcast TV networks started airing a weekly drama called *Kung Fu*, featuring a monk who knew the martial art of kung fu. He would only use his skills for self-defense or to save another person, and no one was ever killed. Each episode included a scene in which the young monk received a lesson from the old master. "Oh, grasshopper," the sage would begin, following with a teaching lifted from Buddhism or from great spiritual leaders, such as Lao Tzu, the founder of Taoism. Stephen declared this to be cool, and a TV was set up in the canning and freezing tent so that folks could watch.

By the mid-1970s, car batteries were providing power for lights in virtually all homes on The Farm, and this same power source could be used to operate small, DC black-and-white televisions. These could be purchased for just over one hundred dollars, and soon many households acquired one. The show *Saturday Night Live* debuted in 1975 with a cast that included John Belushi, Gilda Radner, Dan Aykroyd, and the rest of the Not Ready for Prime Time Players. It was an immediate hit on The Farm. Soon everyone was repeating buzzwords from the show, spouting phrases such as "Well, excuuuse me!" or imitating Steve Martin's frequently seen character, the "wild and crazy guy." That show, which captured the humor and sensibilities of the boomer generation, spoke directly to us. It gave people living on The Farm a way to loosen up and have fun.

Television entered our lives in another way, too. Moms at home with the kids could catch a break by turning on a new show called *Sesame Street*. But since we didn't want to indulge too deeply in mainstream culture, and because battery power was limited, there was a general agreement that we would not expose the kids to Saturday morning cartoon marathons, which were replete with commercials and violent humor.

Music came into our homes as yet another benefit derived from automotive battery power. Car stereos gave each house a sound system, and we often found that listening to rock and roll, reggae, or blues made chores, such as doing the dishes, more fun.

Adding to the blossoming sense of connection to the outside world, in the late 1970s The Farm applied for and received a license for its own FM station, WUTZ. People took turns being DJs, hosting shows, and taking music requests. Every house and workplace had a radio tuned in to the station, so that everyone in the entire community was literally on the same wavelength. As a bona fide station, WUTZ would receive copies of all the newest music releases. This was happening just as new wave and punk hit the world music scene, and the station kept The Farm in sync with contemporary music, providing a way to feel more in touch with hip culture.

Saturday Money

It wasn't long before we realized that the collective economy was not satisfying all of the community's financial needs, especially when it came to the construction of new housing and improvements to existing homes. To alleviate this, members were permitted to work off premises on Saturdays for their own benefit.

This policy change, made in the mid-1970s, gave individuals and households the go-ahead to earn money that did not have to be turned in to the community's central bank. For example, if someone needed funds for a trip to visit family, that person would look for a job outside The Farm that could be done on Saturdays. The work most commonly found was construction and other manual labor for our neighbors.

People who worked on The Construction Crew had an advantage. They were off The Farm every day, and so had more opportunity to meet people who might offer them building projects that could be completed over the course of a couple of Saturdays. These were typically jobs too small for The Farm Building Company to take on but just right for an individual. A crew member, especially a straw boss, might have access to a van and tools, making it easier for him to do the work. If a household had the good fortune to include a few people who worked on The Construction Crew, its potential income could be substantial, enough to purchase building materials for an addition, linoleum for the kitchen floor, a TV—all items that could not be purchased through the regular communal budget.

It was not an equitable system, but it gave people who were willing to take on extra work a way to benefit directly from their efforts. It also helped improve the quality of life for people, making it possible for them to tolerate the shortcomings of the collective income system under which we lived. Stephen used another Bible quote to lend reason to this exception to the rules: "Do not bind the mouths of those that tread the grain."

Sunday Services were one of the essential components that held the community together during those early years. Every Sunday morning, an hour before sunrise, we awakened to the gentle sound of conch shell tones echoing through the ridges and valleys, blown like Gabriel's trumpet announcing that it was time to gather for our weekly meditation. The gentle tones had an earthy resonance that invoked a "primal essence" and amplified the feeling that this weekly ritual connected us to the essential core of our spirituality.

In many ways, the weekly meditation and service by Stephen held on Sunday mornings was the glue that held the community together.

In the dim light of early morning, The Farm's several hundred spiritual seekers would gather in an open meadow that stretched from far up on a hillside all the way down to the creek, and provided a grand vista of the valley below. Across the creek, the ridge lines rose up steeply, a wall of forest across the horizon. The multitudes would sit in silence, listening to the cacophony of birds also rising to greet the day.

With all eyes focused on the upper edge of the tree line, we would watch as the glowing rim of the sun nudged its way into view. Then Stephen would initiate the chanting of "Om," the sound of all voices joined together on a single note, the sound of the universe. It carried the deep resonance of male voices and the pure high notes of the women, with harmonic undertones so sweet and honest that our hearts filled with joy as we felt an unspoken connection to "oneness." The rising energy was pure magic. We would sit, watching the progress of the sun until it would seem to stop, suspended above the trees, and then the "Om," which had rung like church bells for several minutes, would gradually trail off and disappear, leaving our minds and spirits cleansed.

With the energy still high, Stephen would rise and call forward couples who wanted to be married so that we would honor their bond with our most sacred attention before it became mixed with earthly thoughts. In Zen-like form, the wedding vows were stripped down to a bare simplicity. There was no need for Stephen to ramble on about the sanctity of marriage or the relevance of the ceremony. This was considered self-evident. Marriage was the essence of family and symbolized the union that made life itself possible for every person on the planet. Over the next decade, dozens of couples would make the solemn commitment before their friends, before their community, and to the universe in the open expanse reaching up to the heavens.

With these important matters now complete, Stephen would give the signal to "circle up" and all would move in closer to hear him speak. Most of The Farm's residents had been raised in Christian or Jewish traditions, and so the idea of listening to a spiritual figurehead delivering a weekly message was familiar.

That's how I made sense of it. My family had attended a Southern Baptist church, so I regarded Stephen as our preacher delivering a Sunday sermon. It was important to me that I was not under the spell of a cult leader but saw myself as someone committed to following a spiritual path, searching for knowledge and guidance to become a better person.

During the very first years, in winter months when it was too cold to sit outside, Sunday meditation was held in the horse barn, one of the original buildings near The House. In this setting, philosophical debates took place between Stephen and local fundamentalist preachers who would come out to The Farm in an attempt to save our souls. In general, the discussions were carried on in a friendly manner, and there was often humor sprinkled into the conversations. While no minds were converted on either side, these talks helped introduce the community to local Tennesseans, and they spread the word that we were indeed a spiritual community.

As the group grew in size, Sunday Services moved to a larger barn built by the community for The Farming Crew, and then to an even larger and more open building, a greenhouse, which was out of service for the winter.

Of course, there were times when it was just too cold or the weather was too nasty for people to be out and about. In order for the community to continue receiving Stephen's weekly address, one of The Farm's technical engineers came up with a system that modulated Stephen's voice onto the phone lines hooked up to each home. All we had to do then was to place a transistor radio adjacent to the phone and tune it to the right frequency. By this simple method, Stephen's voice could be heard, supplying the unifying connection that helped hold us together through the dark and bitter cold.

Taking this one step further, Farm technicians were able to make use of a lucky find at the county dump. They had discovered that a local cable TV company had discarded miles of aluminum jacketed cable, along with the amplifiers, connectors, and other components for a private TV system. This treasure trove was immediately collected and brought to The Farm, where our technicians used it to build our in-house system by stringing the cable alongside The Farm phone lines were strung on telephone poles and, where there were no poles, in trees. Eventually some 60 percent of Farm households were hooked up to the closed-circuit network. With our own cable system, Stephen could deliver a talk to the community every Sunday morning through the winter, no matter the weather. The system would ultimately be used to broadcast other programs too, such as skits put on by the teenagers attending The Farm School and reports given by those in charge of various aspects of the community.

All Together

By the late 1970s, The Farm's energy was undeniable. With more than one thousand members, the community was like a beehive, with worker bees buzzing about in all directions. Tractors, cars, and trucks constantly moved up and down the main road, but altogether there were only about one hundred vehicles, and those were used mostly by work crews, The Midwives, and the few small businesses. Most people walked or rode a bicycle, which created a steady stream of bodies in motion during most hours of the day.

Even the airwaves crackled from the chatter on CB radios that had been installed in just about every one of our vehicles so that drivers could talk to one another as they traveled the community's byways. In addition, The Farm was actively engaged in amateur radio, which gave those residents with the proper license a way to communicate for free across vast distances. These ham radios were used by our members to stay in touch with Stephen and the band when they were on the road and to keep in contact with people living at the various affiliated satellite communities. By this time, Stephen's appeal had helped to generate a number of smaller communes whose members, hippies and seekers like us who recognized Stephen as a spiritual teacher, were linked in a network under the umbrella of The Farm.

With more than a dozen communities scattered throughout the United States and Canada, along with one in Ireland, The Farm was more than the world's largest commune. Now it was a movement.

SIX

The Satellite Farm

By the early 1970s, The Farm community had begun to feel growing pains. Our population had swelled from the original three hundred to more than six hundred people in just a couple of years. So that we could assimilate the many new people who had already been welcomed into the community, Stephen would occasionally announce that The Gate was closed: no new members would be accepted for a period of time. Those who were turned away were forced to look elsewhere.

During this same period, thousands of small hippie communes were popping up like mushrooms after a rain. The basic hippie philosophy espoused by Stephen and The Farm resonated deeply with people throughout the counterculture and those creating a communal lifestyle in the back-to-the-land movement. In many parts of the country, groups of people who felt a close affinity to The Farm model of community would declare their intention to affiliate and become officially linked with us as part of a developing network of small communities united behind a common philosophy and organizational structure.

At times The Farm would intentionally create a community to fulfill a specific mission or establish a presence in a particular part of the country. Cities were often selected for these Farm offshoots to position our workforce closer to the streams of revenue. Life on the satellite Farms is an important element of Farm history and an integral part of the story.

Rocky Branch

Soon after arriving in Tennessee, Farm members rented and established communal homes in Nashville, where they would live while learning trades, such as construction or printing. They would ultimately bring these skills back home to help establish The Farm's infrastructure and to launch the community's own publishing company. This arrangement was a bit different from the satellite or affiliate communities because it was easy for people to live in Nashville for a while and then return to The Farm. There was a strong connection between those who were temporarily housed in Nashville and the rest of the community at our base in Summertown.

But in a satellite community, far from Stephen and The Farm, the relationship was much different. Sometimes the only link those smaller communes outside of Summertown had to Stephen and The Farm had been forged during a single encounter or by following Stephen's teachings through books and cassette tapes. To enhance the connection between a distant community and the home base, there was a general understanding that a satellite community should include people who had lived on The Farm for a while.

Frequently, when the members of a smaller satellite felt themselves growing more connected to The Farm in Summertown, the pull would become so strong that the group would sell its land and move en masse to the main community. Each influx brought with it a surge of energy—a fresh crop of dedicated new members who brought with them a variety of personal strengths and skills. Absorbing other communities into The Farm populace could also provide a chunk of cash. That happened when money from the sale of the Colorado and West Virginia satellite Farms enabled us to purchase the 750 acres adjoining the original thousand acres, nearly doubling the Tennessee community's land base.

One of the first small communes to proclaim itself a satellite community was a hundred-acre slice of paradise in the mountains of eastern Kentucky called the Rocky Branch Farm. This community had been started by a man named Dan who had used a small inheritance to purchase a tract of land that included a boulder-strewn stream, which gave the community its name. Dan was the brother of a prominent member of the Tennessee Farm, a woman named Cornelia, and that connection gave his place legitimacy. It was also within easy reach of The Farm, about a four-hour drive, making it a logical next stop for those who had been turned away from Summertown when the gates were closed.

Dan was a quiet, unassuming guy, and he opened his doors to those seeking a place to live among the like-minded and a way to join The Farm. In a short time the population at Rocky Branch rose to about twenty people, including two couples from Summertown, who'd moved there and in a sense represented the ways of The Farm and Stephen's teachings.

Unfortunately this became a handicap for Rocky Branch. As it turned out, it seemed to me as if the two men who had come from Summertown were seeking to escape the greater scrutiny of Stephen and others on The Farm. Now, off on their own, they could let their egos rule unchecked, and they were even able to command authority because they had come from the main community. A significant number of the other residents at Rocky Branch were single or newly formed couples, which in Farm hierarchy did not give them the same level of leadership as the couples from Tennessee.

When Rocky Branch was less than a year old, Deborah and I visited it in our search for a small farm to relocate our family. I was aware that at least one of our members known for his temper had moved to Rocky Branch, and while I visited there I was surprised to see him in a leadership role. That made me question whether this was the right place for Deborah and me and our new baby.

Rocky Branch was pretty far up in the mountains, hours away from any major cities, which meant that economic opportunities were limited. As the name implies, this was not fertile farmland. Still, the group at Rocky Branch worked toward their goal of self-sufficiency. They acquired a small tractor and other equipment to work the land, and they planted gardens.

The only building on the property was a large barn, and this became the living quarters. In one corner, a cement slab was poured to form a kitchen floor. In the upper level of the barn, loose planks were stretched across open spaces to function as sleeping platforms, and makeshift walls were established by tacking colorful bedspreads between these areas, affording the semblance of separate bedrooms. Naturally, one of the first tasks was to begin gathering building materials so that the interior of the barn could be converted into adequate communal housing. Work crews began taking on demolition jobs in the nearby small town, tearing down structures and returning each night with salvaged lumber.

Rocky Branch was in possession of a school bus that had been converted into a flatbed truck by cutting away three-quarters of the body at the rear and leaving just the cab with the driver's seat and one extra seat for passengers. The floor of the bus became the bed of the truck, perfect for hauling big loads. It was modeled after a similar bus conversion we had in Summertown.

One of the demolition crew members was a young man named Michael. He and his wife, Susan, had joined Rocky Branch after visiting

Summertown. Michael was a big, burly guy with a bit of a gruff manner, but with a warm smile and a good sense of humor. Built for physical work, he naturally gravitated to the task of demolition.

One job this crew took on involved razing a house in a nearby town. After a particularly long work day, the crew prepared to leave the site and filled the flatbed with lumber they would use at Rocky Branch. There wasn't enough room for everyone in that day's work crew to fit in the cab, so Michael and a couple of other guys climbed on top of the load of lumber for the ride back.

The work crew members were young, naive, and inexperienced, and they made the decision not to strap or chain down the load of materials, certain that the weight of the wood would keep everything in place for the ride home. As the driver maneuvered slowly through the narrow and winding mountain roads, an impatient motorist stuck behind the truck passed at the first opportunity. As the car sped by in the other lane, its motion produced a suction that exerted a pull on the load of wood. The boards shifted and all at once the entire load—along with the crew members sitting on top—came tumbling off the back of the truck in a thunderous crash.

Emergency crews rushed to the scene and transported the guys who had fallen out of the truck to a nearby hospital for evaluation. They were shaken up and a bit beaten up, but everyone seemed to be okay. One fellow had banged up his arm pretty badly but was released from the hospital. Everyone except one crew member was sent home; only Michael was kept behind. Having received the worst of the fall, he was being held overnight for observation. The call came a few hours later. Michael had died.

"The news hit me pretty hard," recalled one of the other members on that crew, a man named Stephen, a tall Texan who had moved to Rocky Branch a few months earlier. "I was planning to sit on the back, but Michael offered me his seat inside the cab. It could have easily been me instead of him."

Deborah and I knew Michael and Susan. They had spent a couple of nights with us when we lived at The Farm in Tennessee. As soon as we heard about the accident, we drove over to Rocky Branch from our home at the time on another satellite commune called the Green River Farm, which was also in Kentucky.

Michael's parents came about a day later. Their son was laid to rest in an old church cemetery on the side of a hill on the Rocky Branch property. It seemed fitting that he should remain with the land, where he had begun to live out his dream.

The incident sent shock waves through the Rocky Branch community and brought on a somber period. Looking back on it now, I believe that Rocky Branch never really recovered from this tragedy. Within about a year, Dan and several others decided to move to the big Farm in Tennessee. The rest of the group simply went back on the road, and the land was put up for sale.

The service for Michael at the Rocky Branch Farm. I'm the eighth person from the left in the row standing; Deborah is seated below me.

In the months after the accident, Susan joined other members of Rocky Branch who went to work at a nearby mental health facility, earning money to support their community. One of those working there was Stephen, the tall Texan. A friendship developed. When Rocky Branch shut down in the fall of 1975, the newly engaged couple moved a few hours west to join Deborah and me on The Green River Farm.

Green River

Unlike Rocky Branch, perched high in the mountains, The Green River Farm was located on sixty acres of Kentucky bottomland stretching all the way down to the Green River itself. Clyde and Christine had moved down from Ohio and bought the land with the dream of establishing a self-sufficient homestead. When Christine became pregnant in the fall of 1974, the couple came to see The Midwives at The Farm in Tennessee.

At that time, Deborah and I were living in a small cabin we'd built. One end opened into a Railway Express truck fixed up as a bedroom, and we were able to take in occasional guests. We hit it off right away with Clyde and Christine.

Since Deborah and I were from Kentucky, Green River appealed to us because we were interested in relocating to a small farm that would be closer to our folks. We were both just twenty years old, the youngest couple on The Farm in Tennessee. Deborah and I loved life on The Farm but felt that a smaller community would offer us more opportunity to take on responsibilities and that in such an environment we'd have more control over our future as a family.

During their short stay with us, Clyde and Christine told us that they wanted their property to become a Farm satellite community. We had already visited Rocky Branch and knew that it wasn't the place for us. In a leap of faith, Deborah and I made the decision to move to Clyde and Christine's farm and help them get their place going. In November of 1974, we hitched a ride to Rocky Branch and then got in touch with Clyde and Christine, asking them to come and pick us up, showing up pretty much unannounced.

There was an old, dilapidated barn on Clyde and Christine's land, but no house. They were living in an abandoned schoolhouse, about a half mile up the road. The largest room in the schoolhouse was in pretty rough shape; its floor had buckled in waves. It was also much too large to heat. Rather than use that for their main living space, Clyde and Christine fixed up the small storeroom in the back, a space about sixteen by thirty feet. The building had electricity, a woodstove for heat, a small gas stove for cooking, and a couple of empty milk cans for hauling water from the shallow well behind the building.

In the back of the room, Clyde and I built two bunk beds. Well, they were more like raised beds. The bed for each couple was about five feet off the ground, which made space underneath for a bed for our newborn son, Jody, and also provided room for storing clothes. For privacy, we were separated from Clyde and Christine's bed by a piece of fabric we'd strung up. It was pretty tight quarters.

A short time after our arrival, Clyde and Christine went down to Tennessee to deliver their baby. Another couple, Cynthia and William, and their baby boy came up from Tennessee and moved into the schoolhouse with us. Living in such close proximity meant that we had to be extremely tolerant and give each other the space necessary to experience life's changes.

For example, when our son Jody was about eight months old, he had the habit of waking up to nurse during the night, crying to let Deborah know he was hungry. However, we felt it was time for him to learn to sleep through the night. He had gained about sixteen pounds since his birth, and Deborah knew he could make it through the night without that extra feeding. We let Cynthia and William know that our plan was to let him cry it out until he went back to sleep. "It might be rough for a few hours!" As expected, Jody woke up and began to cry. His crying went on for a couple of hours, but eventually he did fall back to sleep. From then on, he slept through the entire night. It was well worth the loss of sleep that one night!

Things did not go quite so smoothly for William and Cynthia, but it wasn't baby Benjamin's fault. When it was their turn to try, baby Ben kept crying and crying, and we all noticed that his wail had taken on an increasingly shrill tone. Finally, Cynthia got up to check on him and discovered Benjamin's head covered in blood.

As it turned out, a rat had found its way to Benjamin's crib, most likely en route to nibble some freshly ground cornmeal stored in the house. In the rat's search for food, it had discovered an even more delectable morsel, little Benjamin!

We jumped in our truck and took off for the nearest hospital, which was about fifteen miles away. I drove as fast as I could on the curvy, two-lane country road. Benjamin's bleeding had basically stopped, and we could see little bite marks all across the top of his head. Fortunately, none of the bites were around his face and none were very deep. After a brief check, Benjamin was released from the hospital and we all went back home, a bit shaken, but thankful things were not worse.

However, there was still the task of catching the rat and having it tested for rabies. We set traps, and although we could sometimes hear the rat scurrying about in the night, it never took the bait.

Finally, three nights later, we all awoke to the sound of a loud thud. Willie had heard the rat under his bed, and in a burst of rage and energy, he'd flung a large, heavy round of firewood toward the sound and smashed the rat flat. The suspense was over. Fortunately for little Benjamin, the rat did not have rabies.

Over the course of the summer, down on the land, we finished building a small main house and a couple of extra cabins that functioned as bedrooms. The main house had electricity, but it did not have running water. Unfortunately, the well up at the schoolhouse had become contaminated by waste that had leached from the nearby outhouse, so we had to haul water from a spring about five miles away. That spring was a favorite place for many of the locals to collect their drinking water.

Also that summer, The Farm in Tennessee had again closed its gates to new members, which delivered an influx of new people to Green River. A handful stayed, bringing the group total to twenty-five, then settling down to around fifteen residents.

It felt good to be on the land. We built the house and cabins in the midst of a grove of massive, virgin beech trees; each tree trunk was close to three feet in diameter. It gave the place a magical feel.

The Green River Farm. Deborah, wearing glasses, is on the right in the second row, next to our son, Jody, and then me.

A couple of farmers who lived just down the road took a liking to us and would stop by to visit every day. Howard was in his seventies and had lived in the area all his life. One day he told us, "Boys, people don't live down in the bottoms." It took another year for us to fully understand what he meant.

Although Green River was not in the mountains, it was still a three-hour drive to the nearest big city. Paying jobs in our local area were scarce. Almost everyone at Green River was in their early twenties and had no real skills. I took a job for a while as a helper for a hot-tar roofing company. Another fellow signed up as a welder for a factory making farm gates. For both of us, as the lone hippie working with a bunch of locals, we felt isolated. It certainly was not the atmosphere we had imagined for ourselves when we originally followed our dreams of living off the land.

Clyde's role at Green River was to be the head farmer, and our collective goal was to support The Green River Farm community growing cash crops. We planted seven acres of sweet corn and it did well. When it was ripe and ready to sell, we filled the bed of a pickup with ears of corn, and two of us would drive about an hour to the nearest medium-sized town. There we parked outside of a sewing factory and sold the corn from the back of the truck. The women who worked there would come out to buy our luscious corn on their lunch break. The going price was a dollar a dozen.

It was exciting. The women would pour out in a big wave and overwhelm us. We were bagging corn and grabbing dollars as fast as we could. At the end of the lunch break, we counted up the money. It was about one hundred dollars.

When I thought about all the hours we spent preparing the soil, planting, weeding, and then finally picking and selling the corn, it was clear we weren't making any real money, just pennies an hour. It was pretty discouraging.

The second year on the land, it rained . . . a lot. In front of the main house there was a meandering slough, more of a drainage ditch than a creek. Up until then, it had been completely dry during the year, but it stayed wet all that summer. The constant humidity meant there were a lot of mosquitoes in the standing water. The bottomland leading to the river became oversaturated, raising the water table to only about two feet below ground. We needed to wear rubber boots to trudge through the muck around the houses and out in the fields. The fields became so wet that many of the crops wouldn't grow. Some of the cabins began to sink.

To strengthen their connections with the main Farm in Tennessee and to maintain a regular dialogue, the growing number of satellite Farms were encouraged to have a community member become a licensed ham radio operator. Four of our group, myself included, began studying for our licenses, taking classes in town from a local ham operator. One member of our group, Stephen, who also had previously been at the Rocky Branch Farm, showed the greatest aptitude and was given the go-ahead to study full time. Everything changed the day he got his license.

It was a thrill to be on the air, talking with people at the main Farm and the other Farms, being part of the bigger conversation. Suddenly it became apparent to us at The Green River Farm that we were getting nowhere and struggling just to survive on that land. If our goal was to change the world, it wasn't going to happen there. As a group, we decided we were ready to move on.

Within about a week, a date was set to auction off the land and anything that could bring in some money—the small tractor, furniture, even a broken antique rocking chair. In this way, we raised the funds to pay off Clyde and Christine's note on the land, and there was enough money left to move to the next destination, the New York Farm.

The New York Farm

Clyde and Christine had a connection with several people who were living on an established satellite Farm in upstate New York, and they suggested that after selling off the property, we contribute any remaining assets to the New York Farm. About fifteen of us made the journey, bringing the New York community a decent-running Toyota sedan, a pickup truck in good shape, and a flatbed truck loaded with canned goods and tools.

Although it was a three-hour drive from Manhattan, the New York Farm was situated in an area significantly more affluent than our farm in rural Kentucky. Several of the guys living on the New York Farm had construction skills, and they developed a thriving building and remodeling company, which brought in a good income and easily covered the community's living expenses.

The New York Farm was at the upper end of a long valley, providing a fantastic view of the land below for several miles. Two main houses had come with the land. The residents had built a number of small cabins to serve as bedrooms, but bathroom, kitchen, and laundry facilities were all situated in the larger dwellings. A few house trailers had been brought onto the land as well. A large barn on the property was used as a mechanics' shop, and because the barn had a root cellar, it also was the storage house for winter vegetables. There was enough cleared, flat land for vegetable gardens, and the woods had a grove of sugar maples for syrup production in early spring.

Our contingency from Kentucky arrived on Christmas Day 1976. Deborah and I had never been to this part of the country; it was a new experience for us to be in a land covered by snow for months at a time. Everyone was very welcoming, and the community had a warm and inviting vibe. However, it wasn't long before the winter enchantment wore off and we longed for a warmer climate. It became clear to us that our real desire was to get back to Tennessee.

The New York Farm stayed active for many years, shutting down in the early 1980s. Several factors led to its dissolution, including friction among residents and disputes between community members and community leaders.

It would seem that many on the New York Farm also longed for warmer climes, because a large contingent moved to Gainesville, Florida. There, the former members of the New York Farm established a new construction business, this time with a clear organizational structure delineating owners, partners, and employees. Other former New York Farm members moved to the Gainesville area but found different means of employment, still drawn to the friendships and sense of community that remained intact by the shared bond of the New York Farm experience.

The Florida Farm

Unlike most small Farms in the network of satellite communities, The Florida Farm was created as a project of The Farming Crew in Tennessee. In order to practice their newly gained skills year-round, The Farming Crew began leasing land south of Miami, in Homestead, Florida, growing vegetables in the winter months that could be shipped up to Tennessee.

The Florida Farm also became a place to earn money. Initially this was to help fund the operating expenses of The Farming Crew. Work at a green-bean-packing house was so lucrative that it became a revenue stream for the main Farm in Tennessee, and eventually more than one hundred people were dispatched to Florida to work all the plant's shifts.

Several places were rented near Homestead to provide communal housing for The Farm folks working at the packing plant and the additional support team. The population of this crew ebbed and flowed with the change of seasons. The Chrome House, on a busy highway called Chrome Avenue, was home to twenty people, including an eccentric homeless man in his seventies someone had "rescued" when he was discovered wandering about the local Greyhound bus station. The Pool House, named for its inground pool at the back patio, was situated about five miles farther south in a more suburban neighborhood. In addition to the large main house, this property included a separate row of what appeared to be motel rooms that were also used as bedrooms. A couple of army tents and several plywood cabins were set up, providing living quarters for about thirty-five people.

Single people or couples without children stayed at an abandoned migrant labor camp in the middle of a lime orchard that we also rented closer to the leased agricultural fields. This camp housing had electricity, a central kitchen building, bathrooms, and showers, but because of the crude living conditions, the rent was relatively inexpensive. Altogether, the array of dwellings allowed the population at The Florida Farm to swell during green bean season, which coincided with the winter months in Tennessee when there was little for The Farming Crew to do there anyway.

Once this system had been established, it became more practical for the community as a whole to keep some people in Florida year-round rather than start over seeking new rentals every season. The Florida Farm soon took on another purpose, that of a healing center. One man who was a paraplegic and another with cerebral palsy moved there to escape Tennessee's winters and to bask in the warmth of the south Florida sun. Even a bad back that refused to heal could be sufficient grounds for a member to put in a request for a stay in Florida.

To support the Florida community and pay the rent on the various locations, a team of roofers started working and bringing in a good income. A few others found local jobs. Once it was deemed an official satellite community, residents of The Florida Farm were selected at the main Farm to fulfill particular skilled roles. For instance, there was a mechanic to maintain the growing fleet of vehicles and several trained medical people to operate an in-house clinic.

I was sent down in the winter of 1977 to serve as the ham radio operator. I had passed the exam in Tennessee for a General license, but I still needed to acquire an Advanced Class license in order to gain access to the frequencies that The Farm's radio team were using. In Tennessee the licensing tests were only given a few times a year, but in Florida the tests could be taken every week. My family and I moved to Florida, where I did some final studying, and a few weeks later I took and passed the Advanced test. We stayed on a few more months, basically through the winter, but we were eager to get back to Tennessee. Life on The Florida Farm felt to us very much like living in a city. What's more, the water in Homestead tasted awful.

The transplanted Tennessee Farming Crew had undertaken a new business: commercial farming. The crew rented large fields in Florida to grow green beans to sell on the open market. At the height of the Florida farming operation, a freak blast of cold air sent freezing temperatures south of Miami all the way to Homestead. The Farming Crew's crop was devastated, and a loss estimated at $100,000 was accrued over the course of a single night. Leaders of The Farming Crew and the community's financial managers were in shock. This signaled the end of commercial farming endeavors. Soon enthusiasm for the work at the green-bean packing-plant began to fade as well.

After a few years, with farming no longer the central activity, the relevance of the Florida Farm diminished. Its population shrank as people drifted back up to the main Farm in Tennessee, and eventually The Florida Farm shut down for good.

The California Farm

With so many connections to California, it seemed logical that The Farm would have a satellite community there. However, probably because Stephen's followers from California who wanted to be part of The Farm's efforts had moved with him to Tennessee, a California satellite had never developed. Discussions began in the late 1970s and plans were initiated to establish a presence in the Bay Area. A group was sent out from the main Farm to open a soy dairy that would produce and sell tofu as a cottage industry. Needless to say, the cost of living on the West Coast was quite high, and launching a new business with no real startup capital proved to be extremely difficult. Various locations were tried, but after several years the effort was abandoned.

In a sense, the trial and error of life in the satellite communities was a training ground for The Farm's next phase, the one many would say was the true expression of what the whole experiment was all about.

SEVEN

Plenty: Because There Is Enough, If We Share

By the mid-1970s, The Farm was feeling pretty strong. The Farming Crew was able to provide most of the food needed to feed everybody. The Farm Building Company was well established and employed close to one hundred men, who produced a steady income for the community. Still, something was missing. The real mission had never been to create the ultimate hippie commune but to make a difference, to push idealism to the limits, as in the words of our slogan displayed across the front of our Greyhound bus: "Out to save the world."

Giving Back

We all understood that The Farm and the hippie movement were products of America's middle class. Most of us were white kids, the benefactors of European colonialism that had been exploiting the rest of the world for the last several centuries, exterminating native cultures, and plundering the world's resources. Now spiritually aware and socially conscious, we understood that our generation had a shared responsibility. It was our job to assist those people who had not benefited as we had. Given our position, we felt it only correct that we should help those who had been denied access to what we believed were basic human rights: clean water, adequate food, shelter, education, better health, and medical care.

The first discussions along this line of thinking took place at Sunday Services while Stephen was still in the penitentiary but able to come home on weekends. We were aware of the crippling impact poverty and hunger could have on a culture, and in our effort to show solidarity with those folks, every member of The Farm signed a Vow of Poverty. We were living on about a dollar a day. Pretty much everything any of us wore was a hand-me-down. We were dedicated and committed to making a difference in the lives of everyone on the planet. But it seemed time to do more than talk about changing the world; we had to do something about it.

We believed that if the world's resources were distributed equitably, there would be enough for everyone. Not just enough but an abundance, plenty. And so in 1974, The Farm established our first nonprofit and named it Plenty. The next step was to raise the periscope, look around, and—like a superhero—jump into the fray to see where we could help. It made sense to start out close to home.

As Farm residents started getting better educated about the issues surrounding hunger and need, we learned that some established local soup kitchens and food banks had been shut down. These had been set up during the previous decade, under President Johnson's War on Poverty, and they had been located in neighborhoods in Memphis and in Lawrenceburg, which happened to be just down the road from us. Unfortunately, when the Nixon administration came into power, these resources were closed. We started hauling some of our extra sweet potato crop into these neighborhoods and distributing food to the people there.

A tornado touched down in nearby Alabama, and members of The Farm were dispatched to help in the cleanup efforts. While engaged in this work, our volunteers hooked up with folks from the Mennonite Central Committee. Soon after, the committee made a contract with Plenty to purchase black beans to supply Cuban refugees in South Florida, where a hurricane had struck.

The Mennonite Central Committee was involved in projects all over the world, including Honduras and Haiti, and the members of The Farm directly involved with Plenty began to realize the vast scope of work that could be done to help those in need.

The Land of Eternal Spring

Early one morning in February 1976, members of The Farm's Radio Crew were listening in on the airwaves when they heard distress calls coming out of Guatemala, where a violent earthquake had destroyed virtually all telephone lines and standard forms of communication. Because the earthquake occurred in the middle of the night when most people were sleeping, many had been killed under the collapsing walls of their adobe homes. More than twenty-five thousand people had died, hundreds of thousands were left homeless, and the country's infrastructure was in shambles.

Understanding the urgency, The Farm dispatched a woman who spoke Spanish, and who happened to be doing medical work at The Farm Clinic, to assess the situation and see if Plenty could be of assistance. One of the first things we learned was that there was not a single EKG machine in Guatemala. All had been destroyed. From our base in Summertown, we contacted all the hospitals in Nashville, asking if there were any extra EKG machines. We learned of a machine available in St. Louis, and a couple of men drove there in a pickup to get it. The EKG unit was put on a plane sent by the Mennonites, along with supplies they were sending to Guatemala.

Our involvement in this project brought an important change in perspective to The Farm community. When The Farm's representatives returned from their travels and gave their report at a Sunday Service, their assessment started a discussion that challenged our communal sense of justice and commitment.

Previously, to express our solidarity as a group and help people understand our way of life, Stephen had begun referring to us as "voluntary peasants." But now our community had to come to terms with the difference between voluntary peasants and involuntary peasants. As individuals who'd chosen this lifestyle, any one of us could have run back to our parents, returned to college, and rejoined America's middle class at any time.

We had come to see that the stakes were much higher for our counterparts in Third World countries. For an involuntary peasant, there is a delicate line between life and death. High infant mortality rates and shorter life spans resulting from a myriad of preventable causes are the hard reality. As one mind, the community was coming to grips with the fact that thousands of people would die unless they received help.

At the same time, The Farm community began to ask itself, "Can we really do global outreach when we don't even have our own infrastructure in place?" Most of the houses on The Farm were still without running water. Many of us were still living in buses and tents.

Despite these self-imposed conditions, we also recognized that compared with much of the world, The Farm was quite rich. There was no doubt that we lived in a land of wealth and abundance. The situation in Guatemala presented us with an opportunity to share our riches, and it was staring us right in the face. It was a chance to give back.

With so many homes destroyed and people displaced in Guatemala, it seemed clear that one of the most important ways Plenty could help was by building houses. Right away several of our carpenters and their tools were flown to Guatemala, even though they weren't quite sure what they were going to do when they got there. Almost by chance, The Farm's carpenters ran into someone who suggested they go to the Canadian Embassy. There, they were introduced to the Canadian ambassador, who told them that a freighter was on its way, loaded with over one hundred tons of building materials, such as fiberboard, lumber, roofing tin, hammers, and nails. There were no plans for what to do with the materials once they arrived. The Farm's lead carpenter started drawing on a piece of paper, and after a couple of minutes, he handed the paper back to the ambassador with one design for a house and another for a school. An agreement was made on the spot for Plenty to take charge of the distribution and utilization of the building materials.

San Andrés Itzapa, a small town about an hour outside the capital, Guatemala City, had been almost entirely destroyed and was identified as an ideal location for our builders to get started. The materials were dropped off at a soccer field. Farm carpenters established work crews to fabricate walls and roof trusses at a central location. These components could then be assembled and nailed together on-site for each home. Because the townspeople had no previous experience with this type of construction, we trained the local Mayan volunteers to use the tools and then we taught them the basics of wood frame building. Altogether, Plenty and the Guatemalan helpers built more than twelve hundred homes in this one village.

Now with a proven track record, Plenty's partnership with the Canadian government continued. We moved on to build schools and municipal buildings. Back on The Farm in Tennessee, the excitement grew for our project abroad as more and more people were dispatched to work in Guatemala. The support team was expanded to include mechanics to keep the construction vehicles moving, people to cook and manage the base camp, and folks with medical experience to keep everyone healthy and functioning. By the second year, the camp's population had grown to more than one hundred.

When word in the Mayan villages began to spread that there were people with medical skills as well as medicine among the Plenty volunteers, the sick and dying began arriving at our camp for help. The most heartbreaking to see were the infants who suffered from dysentery and malnutrition. Not all survived, but many were nursed back to health with not much more than tender loving care and a little soy milk administered through an eyedropper.

As Plenty's reputation to perform medical miracles grew, the demand for assistance increased exponentially. One of the construction vehicles was commandeered to serve exclusively as an ambulance. Volunteers from The Farm, who had no formal education other than basic training at The Farm Clinic, were energized by their ability to save lives.

Unfortunately, their efforts did not receive a warm welcome from the Guatemalan government. Plenty volunteers were authorized to do construction, not to offer medical care. Their dedicated service to the poor and often marginalized Mayan people began to appear in stark contrast to the less-than-stellar medical services provided by the government. Issues of power and authority came into play. Now, two years after the disaster, the situation was no longer one of mass chaos, and Plenty's helpful work behind the scenes had turned to an annoying blip on the radar screen of local authorities. In order to continue working, Plenty agreed to stop all medical service and moved our base of operations deeper into the Guatemalan highlands to the town of Sololá, a three-hour drive from Guatemala City.

Lake Atitilán

We rented a large home with several outbuildings and a few acres of land on the outskirts of Sololá to serve as Plenty's new headquarters in Guatemala. The house had electricity and running water, but the ten-foot-high, plastered adobe walls of the home were laced with cracks from the earthquake, and so it wasn't considered safe for living quarters. Instead the crew, now down to about forty people, slept in the outbuildings and in small cabins constructed from some of the leftover building materials. The plan was to use the house strictly for its facilities, including a kitchen and dining area, an office, and hangout space.

The house was perched on land some seven thousand feet above sea level and about one thousand feet above Lake Atitilán, which is one of the largest high-elevation lakes in the world. From our vantage point, Lake Atitlán was a bright blue jewel several miles across. It is surrounded by three volcanoes along the lakeshore, and two more were visible to us, way off in the distance. The altitude kept tropical temperatures at bay, and it felt like springtime all year long. Mayan farmers grew large plots of vegetables along the terraced mountainsides. We were truly enchanted by the climate and the people, surrounded as we were by the Mayan families, who were radiant in their colorful handwoven clothing and whose ancient dialects lilted through the air.

To coincide with the move, Plenty took on one of its most ambitious projects to date, again stepping just outside the lines of normal reconstruction projects.

As members of The Farm began to learn about the culture of Guatemala, we saw that the population of the country was about 80 percent indigenous Mayan people, who were controlled by the 20 percent of the population who were of Spanish descent and were descendants of the original colonial powers. The government, the land, and the entire economy were in the hands of this minority. As Plenty's volunteers came to better understand the ways of the Mayan people, we learned that the Mayan communities had continued to maintain their own system of government, which empowered village elders, known as *alcaldes*, to arbitrate disputes and make decisions for their villages.

Plenty came up with the idea to construct a municipal building to serve as a central meeting place for the elders, and built it on the town square, directly across the street from the state government building. The Indigenous Municipal, or *Municipalidad Indígena*, had a dual purpose: As an edifice, it provided a solid presence that was meant to empower the Mayan people of Sololá, and it could also help them preserve their culture in the face of Western domination. On the second floor of this building, in addition to the offices and meeting rooms, Plenty installed an FM broadcasting station, making it possible for the Mayan people to communicate in their own native languages.

A half dozen small storefronts, little *tiendas*, were set up around the exterior of the building. The proprietors rented their spaces, thereby providing income for the building, which helped fund its upkeep. The building's location placed it at the center of the town's biweekly marketplace, a focal point for the international tourism that has played a vital role in Guatemala's economy.

Deborah and I were among those sent down to Sololá in what could be regarded as the second phase of volunteers from The Farm. My primary motivation for acquiring my amateur radio license was so that I could travel to the Third World and serve on a Plenty project. Deborah had trained in The Farm Clinic as a lab technician and had learned to use a microscope to identify parasites and do blood work to track infections.

We both had skills that were considered essential for the team, and we jumped at the chance to go, arriving in December 1978 with our two children, Jody and Leah, ages four and two. Our time in Guatemala turned out to be one of the defining experiences of our lives.

As Plenty matured as an organization, its directors began to recognize many ways the earlier medical work we'd done had been more about treating symptoms than about finding solutions to endemic problems. Medical emergencies like dysentery were the result of unclean water and poor sanitation. The Mayan people were typically small and short in stature, not because of genetic differences from their North American or European

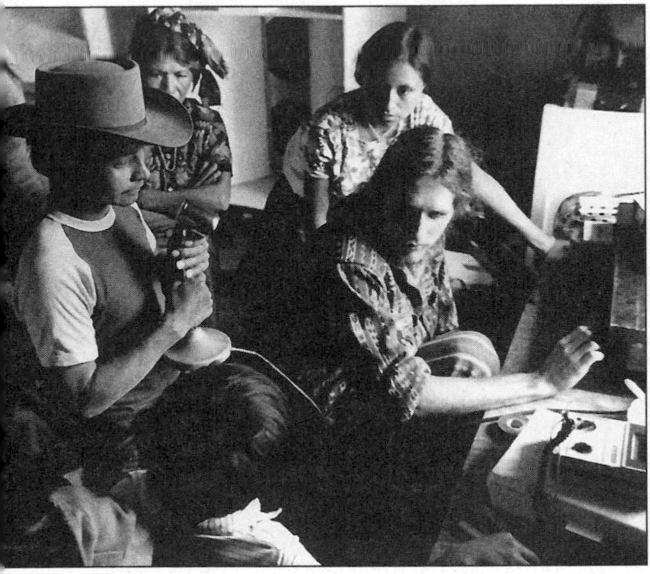

Left: As the project's ham radio operator, I helped families in Guatemala stay in touch with their loved ones receiving training back on The Farm in Tennessee. Right: Deborah's role as our lab technician in Guatemala was to monitor parasites in our drinking water and in our volunteers.

counterparts, but because of malnutrition. If it was to create lasting change, Plenty's work would need to address the root causes of such problems.

At The Farm we had discovered how soy milk and soy foods could improve the health and well-being of children and adults. With that in mind, Plenty began to explore ways to introduce the noble soybean into the local diet. Several farmers were sent down from Tennessee to conduct trials and see which types and varieties of soy would grow best in the climate and altitude of the Guatemalan highlands. Plenty volunteers with experience in the preparation of soy foods began hosting demonstrations in the villages surrounding the camp.

Rural Mayan villages of the late 1970s did not have electricity, and the gasoline mill for grinding corn had not yet been introduced there. Mayan women would grind corn by hand, just as their ancestors had done for centuries, on a large stone called a *metate*. The Plenty volunteers conducting the soy demos were able to grind the soaked soybeans by exactly the same method. The ground soy pulp was then added to a pot of water and cooked over the fire. Next the liquid was strained through a cheesecloth, removing the pulp, and cups of hot soy milk sweetened with a little sugar were passed around for all to try. Next, a little lemon juice was added, which transformed the liquid into curds and whey. The high-protein curds, or soy cheese, better known as tofu, were flavored with a little seasoning, and everyone got to taste a sample.

Plenty volunteers gave out samples of soy ice cream, or "ice bean," at schools throughout the region.

Taking things one step further, Plenty's people working on the soy project acquired a machine for making soft-serve ice cream. The typical ice cream served in the local markets tasted awful. It was full of chemicals and artificial flavoring, and it contained very little milk. In contrast, the soy "ice bean" was rich and creamy, flavored with local fruits, such as mangoes, limes, and blackberries, purchased in the market. Five-gallon buckets of this nutritious dessert were taken to schools throughout the region, and free samples were given to all the children. It was an instant hit!

Impressed by the potential of soy to combat Guatemala's nutrition problems, the Canadian government provided funding for the construction of a soy "dairy" to produce, distribute, and sell soy products. The operation would become a cottage industry for the village of San Bartolo.

To ensure the quality of its products, the soy dairy needed to have clean water. At that time all villagers hauled their water directly from the streams and creeks that flowed down the mountainsides. It was also standard practice for people of the villages to defecate or relieve themselves in the cornfields or behind a wall outside their homes. Consequently, the water in the surrounding streams was polluted, and drinking it was the main cause of the intestinal parasites that plagued almost everyone who drank the local water.

Members of Plenty followed the flow of a stream near the dairy, high up into the mountains to its source. The landowner was then persuaded to donate the water from that spring to the village below. To prevent groundwater contamination, the spring's mouth was encased in cement and plastic pipes were installed for about a half mile to guide and protect the water as it flowed down the mountainside. The water then emptied into a large cement holding tank that had been built for this purpose by Mayan masons hired by Plenty. The village provided volunteers to dig the trenches and lay the additional pipelines, and they installed a water spigot at every home. The entire system relied on the force of gravity. It worked without electricity, pumps, or moving parts that would require future maintenance. The soy dairy had its clean water!

Because the people from the village of San Bartolo were to operate the soy dairy, we needed to educate them about proper sanitation, including the basics, such as the importance of hand washing. In addition to the more formal discussions held at meetings with the villagers, Plenty volunteers performed skits to illustrate their points on this subject. A few cornstalks were placed about the room and two women from Plenty sat on the floor, acting as if they were having a picnic. In came Mr. Fly, dressed in black tights and sporting a pair of wings. Rubbing his hands together like an evil villain, he proclaimed the joys of eating *mierda*, or shit, as he buzzed over to touch the tortillas of the oblivious picnickers. The crowd was in stitches, but the point was made. Soon each home in the village had its own hand-dug latrine covered by a protective cement lid, donated by another organization working in Guatemala.

With fresh water available to the residents of San Bartolo, they could now easily wash their hands, and they had clean water for drinking, for preparing meals, and for bathing. We could see that this was the type of development that could have a lasting impact for the villagers. Inspired by the success of the water project, Plenty looked for places to replicate it.

A few more systems were installed for other small villages, and then an even more challenging opportunity presented itself. We took on a project to develop a system that would serve three villages and a total of ten thousand people—perhaps the most ambitious undertaking of Plenty's time in Guatemala. A local Guatemalan engineer was hired to help develop the plans and ensure the project's success.

Another water project we worked on took place outside Plenty's usual sphere of influence, at a village located several hours on the opposite side of Guatemala City. Because this area was at a lower elevation and had suffered deforestation, it was intensely hot and had become a virtual desert. Without trees on the hillsides to hold the water, the local streams had dried to a mere trickle. Women from the village stood in long lines taking turns at these poorly flowing springs to fill their water jugs, carrying the murky liquid back a mile or more to their families. Desperate village leaders, who had learned of Plenty's work with water, came to us asking for help.

Moved by their plight, Jeremy, one of Plenty's volunteers, hiked through the steep hillsides, searching until he found a spring that could serve the village. After a water source was secured, a truckload of pipe was delivered, and the project began in earnest. During this time, because the location was such a long distance away from our base in Sololá, Jeremy and Plenty's other volunteers lived in the village for a week at a time, sleeping in the storage building that held the pipe and preparing their meals on a portable gas camping stove. One evening, as they were getting ready to cook their supper, someone filled the stove with gas and set the can of fuel off to the side without sealing it shut. After the stove was ignited, the flames quickly followed the vapor trail many feet through the air, until they reached the fuel can. Panicking, Jeremy rushed to grab the burning can of fuel. He carried it outside the building, inadvertently splashing the flaming liquid down his legs. Burning fuel also landed on a foam mattress and set it on fire. Despite Jeremy's efforts, the building and all of the water pipe inside burned to the ground.

Meanwhile, to smother the fire on Jeremy's legs, villagers rolled him in sand. They loaded him into the back of a pickup truck and drove several hours to a hospital in Guatemala City. Although there was an American-style hospital in the city that served the wealthy elite, Jeremy was taken to the general hospital that ministered to the majority of the

Mayan people. Because his wounds were not life-threatening, Jeremy was given a couple of aspirin, placed on a bed, and left in the hallway.

It took many more hours for the other volunteers to get back to Sololá and report the accident. Plenty's medic and I were dispatched immediately to find Jeremy.

We found him delirious with pain, abandoned in the hallway amid the chaos that can be common in urban hospitals. We quickly moved him into our vehicle and took him to the other hospital. Although the villagers had been trying to help, their method of putting out the fire had embedded sand in many of Jeremy's third-degree burns, making the process of cleaning his wounds extremely difficult. After several days, we were able to bring him back to his room in Sololá, where he spent months in recovery. His bandages and dressings had to be changed every day. There was little I could do to help him but to be there as a friend. I would sit with him each day to keep him company and try to take his mind off the pain.

As the months wore on, Jeremy recovered. The water pipe was replaced, and the project was completed. Everyone learned a lot about dedication and sacrifice, perseverance and the strength of human spirit.

Meanwhile things were not going so well in Guatemala, the land of eternal spring. Farther south, in Nicaragua, the brutal dictator Somoza had been driven out by a people's insurrection called the Sandinista National Liberation Front. Just over the border, El Salvador was engaged in a brutal civil war. Guatemala's government, controlled by a series of military dictatorships since a CIA-backed coup had overthrown a progressive, democratically elected civilian government in the mid-1950s, was deeply concerned that it could be the next domino to fall to communist-backed rebels.

During his term, the US Democratic president Jimmy Carter had denied Guatemala's military funding and aid because of its dismal human rights record. When Carter lost his reelection bid in 1980 to Republican Ronald Reagan, the political climate in Guatemala changed almost immediately.

Shortly after the election, due to the Reagan administration's policy that backed and supplied anticommunist forces, military checkpoints began appearing at the roads leading into every major Guatemalan city. Buses headed into the capital were frequently stopped at random points along the highway. Everyone on board was told to get out while soldiers searched for weapons and looked for anyone they considered subversive.

Plenty's camp in Sololá was situated high in the mountains above Lake Atitlán. Much of the mountainous region had no roads accessible by cars or trucks, making it an ideal hideout for the rebel insurgency. As a result, the Guatemalan military's presence in the area increased dramatically. Several new army bases were established there, and helicopters armed with machine guns flew low in the sky over the Plenty camp on a daily basis.

Even more disturbing were the actions of the death squads and the massacres that began to take place weekly throughout the country. Every newspaper contained photos of the body dumps, where slaughtered men, women, and children had been left to rot.

Initially, the death squads left the gringos alone. There was some concern on their part that attacking foreigners would draw the attention of international media and create a public relations problem for the Guatemalan government. Their tactic instead was to go after the Guatemalans working for aid groups, sending a message to outside organizations such as Plenty that their help was no longer wanted.

This was brought home to us starkly one day when the Guatemalan engineer who had been hired to do drawings for our water projects returned to his home after work at the Plenty offices and was approached by his neighbors with grave news. "The death squad was just here looking for you." He quickly gathered up his family and a few possessions and came back to us seeking money to relocate in another part of the country. We felt responsible, that we had endangered the family through his work with Plenty. Of course we gave them whatever funds we could spare.

After the earthquake, the reconstruction effort had been organized as an official project of the Guatemalan government, with its own department and cabinet secretary, a man who was sympathetic to the plight of the poor. This meant that representatives from Plenty were required to make frequent trips to the capital for meetings in government offices, which were often the targets of bombs and firefights.

A number of people we had gotten to know in various parts of the country, our Guatemalan friends, were being accosted by police, had been severely beaten, or had disappeared. Our men, with their long hair and beards, were the symbols of rebellion. Hippies in general were considered subversive. We grew to understand that our very presence endangered our friends.

Stress became a constant undercurrent, and there came a point when we realized our time in Guatemala had come to an end. We were all gathered in the living room on a Saturday night, just hanging out, when the conversation started. It became clear that most of us were feeling very paranoid. I was starting to have bad dreams. We had to recognize the fact that we were there with our kids and didn't feel safe anymore. It was time to go.

Within about a month, Stephen came down with The Farm's Greyhound bus and loaded everyone up for the long ride back to Tennessee. Three men stayed on for a short while to tie up loose ends, but for the most part the projects were ready to stand on their own. Plenty hired a few Guatemalans to maintain continuity and to manage those projects that would need additional attention.

Moving On

Although the work in Guatemala was over, it wasn't the end for Plenty. The organization's directors began to look around to see where they might go next. Two volunteers and their families went to work in Bangladesh. Plenty partnered with the Fri, a sailing vessel manned by hippies from Europe who were making a tour of the Caribbean. A few Plenty volunteers joined the crew, visiting the islands to identify new places where Plenty could continue its work. Projects were started by Plenty volunteers in Jamaica and with the indigenous people on the island of St. Lucia. In 1980, Plenty came to the realization that there were places in the United States with conditions very much the same as in the Third World, including New York's South Bronx.

During a trip to England, Stephen had learned about "squatting," a term used to describe taking over abandoned buildings and houses for living space. Not long after his return to the United States, Stephen heard about a group of squatters in the South Bronx who had established headquarters in an abandoned building for their "urban peacekeeping patrols." They had begun to receive a lot of media attention and their efforts intrigued Stephen. Inspired by this mission, Plenty spread the word that it was looking for volunteers to find an abandoned building and open a city center in the heart of what most of society saw as America's abandoned wasteland.

Seeking a purpose and a mission, the Plenty team decided to open a free ambulance service staffed by people trained on The Farm as emergency medical technicians (EMTs) and paramedics. We had learned that response times from the New York City ambulance service to the South Bronx were dismal, if the ambulances even showed up at all. The area was

Members of The Farm, working as volunteers for the community's nonprofit Plenty, took over an abandoned building to launch a free ambulance service for the people of the South Bronx.

considered too dangerous. Plenty's effort would illustrate that America's urban poor deserved the same level of respect and care as anyone else in the country.

A search party was sent to the city to scout out a location. In short order they found a multistory building and formulated a plan to use the bottom floor for the ambulance service and rooms on the upper floors as living quarters for the crew and their families. With a base of operations established, it wasn't long before a crew of about thirty was in place, with donated ambulances meeting city specifications on call twenty-four hours a day. The effect was instant and obvious. Lives were being saved. Plenty's ambulances were transporting all manner of people to hospitals, from those who'd been shot or stabbed to sick children and the forsaken elderly. The bold move soon garnered its own media attention, with a front-page story in the *Wall Street Journal*, an article in *People* magazine, and prime-time coverage on an NBC news show.

To generate income that could support the operation, volunteers who had construction skills got jobs replacing and retrofitting windows in buildings throughout the city. Keeping the spirit of The Farm alive, the Bronx group had its own rock band, which was composed of extremely talented musicians and singers who would perform on the building's rooftop. The crew even had its own midwife, who delivered babies as an additional service for the people of the Bronx.

Naturally, the crew of mostly middle-class white kids attracted the attention and curiosity of its black and Hispanic neighbors. The operation demonstrated for us and to others that when you treat people with respect, respect will be given. At no time were any of the crew hassled, nor were any of the ambulances vandalized. The Plenty volunteers were very quickly welcomed as an essential part of the community.

Just as they had done on The Farm in Tennessee, crew members began offering classes and training people of the neighborhood to become licensed EMTs. Local volunteers were then able to take shifts as regular members of the ambulance crew. Some who had acquired licenses used their new status to find employment with the official New York City ambulance service. Now staffed with residents from the Bronx, the New York ambulances began responding to calls there. After five years, response times to the South Bronx were on par with what could be expected for any other part of the city. The Plenty ambulance service was able to close its doors.

In 1980, Stephen Gaskin, representing Plenty International, was named one of the first two recipients of the Right Livelihood Award presented at a ceremony in the Swedish Parliament. This internationally recognized and prestigious honor is often referred to as the "Alternative Nobel Prize." Stephen and Plenty were recognized for "caring, sharing, and acting with and on behalf of those in need at home and abroad."

Making a Difference

The Guatemala experience and other work by Plenty represented the peak expression of The Farm's vision. We learned through these efforts what it meant to be truly part of something greater than ourselves.

Before the formation of Plenty and our experience in Guatemala, The Farm was fairly isolated. We didn't read newspapers or watch much TV. Our attention was focused almost exclusively on building the community. Through Plenty, we came to understand the endemic poverty that billions of people around the world endure from cradle to grave, and we saw that the things we had been learning in taking care of ourselves at The Farm—installing water systems, focusing on better nutrition, ensuring our families had good primary medical care, and raising a new standard for childbirth through midwifery—were now skills that we could apply to help others. What's more, these essentials were desperately needed by so much of the world.

At the same time, the people living at the remaining satellite city centers and Plenty projects had no idea of the tremendous turmoil coming to a head back at the mothership in Tennessee. The Farm was on the brink of collapse, and not even those living on the land realized what was about to happen.

EIGHT

The Vow of Poverty

All through the 1970s and into the 1980s, each person who joined the community signed an actual Vow of Poverty. We were committing ourselves to a life of service to humanity, forsaking wealth and riches for a spiritual path in a family monastery that was out to save the world.

As noble as this idea was, after more than ten years of living in this manner, the zeal of idealism was beginning to fade. Our goal had been to have a modest but comfortable lifestyle. Still, even for the most basic level of existence, it takes money to live. As it happened, the vast majority of The Farm's population were inclined to work in service roles inside the community, which generated no income, rather than to find work at ordinary jobs in nearby towns. The community's self-sufficiency plan was to create new businesses, companies of our own. A number were launched, but because our entrepreneurs were short on both experience and investment capital, most of these small startups struggled to stay afloat. They did not put much money into the community budget.

The sum total of all the income generated by members of the community provided no more than a dollar and a half a day for each adult resident of The Farm. Even back then, it was not nearly enough to provide for all of a person's needs, and it clearly wasn't enough to raise a family. The depth of poverty every resident had to endure was amplified by an infrastructure inadequate to fulfill the needs of our expanding population. In many ways, The Farm was an ironic sketch in contrasts, a place where pockets of amazing high tech existed within a world in which basic services were simply patched together and never seemed to be regarded as a priority.

The End of Satellite Farms

The first cracks in our grand plan began to appear when many of The Farm satellite communities were closed, sold, or abandoned, which brought those members living on the fringes of The Farm network back home to Tennessee.

The satellite endeavors ended for many different reasons. The community in Wisconsin could never get on its feet economically, and the harsh winters made basic survival difficult. A small Farm in Missouri had a strong construction company and a population that got along well, but when a nuclear power plant was built within sight of the community, no one wanted to continue living there. The pull back to the main Farm in Tennessee was strong. As one by one most of the satellite communities folded, their members were absorbed into the already crowded housing at the Summertown Farm.

To help launch the satellite communities and city centers, The Farm had often dispatched its strong leaders, people with the charisma and energy to get things done, who we called manifestors. These people not only would organize the various efforts but also would serve to ensure that each new community had a direct tie to The Farm's philosophy and Stephen's teachings. As the 1970s came to a close, and with the community in Tennessee struggling, Stephen and others felt it best to bring these folks back and consolidate energy.

In the fall of 1980, with the political climate of Guatemala becoming increasingly volatile, Plenty International shut down operations there and brought its forty or so volunteers and their families back to the main Farm, which was then a community bursting at the seams and struggling to survive. In a sense, the Guatemala project was also like a satellite community, another outpost of The Farm's skilled and talented members who were called home.

Returning to The Farm after being in Guatemala for almost two years was a bit of a shock for me. The population on The Farm had increased substantially but not much else had changed, at least in terms of housing and infrastructure. It was clear that there was not enough money flowing in. There was a tension in the air as those of us returning from Guatemala struggled to take up where we had left off. It was becoming increasingly obvious that despite the community's best efforts, things were not coming together the way we had imagined.

The Farm's population was now at an all-time high, somewhere between twelve hundred and fifteen hundred people, all of us crowded into half-finished houses. Each house was filled with four or five families as well as an assortment of single people, and some dwellings had as many as fifty residents. Here we were ten years into the project and many people were still living in a couple of dozen army tents and crude shacks. Most of the original school buses were still occupied as well, often being used as an external bedroom associated with a larger household. To add instant housing, a number of used house trailers were purchased with funds that had come in from the liquidated satellite communities. Compared to the buses, tents, and unfinished homes, the trailers felt pretty uptown. But they were often used to house more than one family, and because they had been poorly built from lesser-grade materials, the trailers did not hold up well. They quickly deteriorated, adding to our impoverished appearance.

Inadequate Infrastructure

The Farm was sinking under the weight of inefficiency, a modus operandi referred to tongue-in-cheek on The Farm as a "temporary necessary expediency." Because we were short on money but awash in unpaid labor, we were able to have our crews establish many impractical systems that became the status quo.

When the land was purchased, it had one small house, a couple of barns, a well, and a network of logging roads that snaked through the property. The Farm's primary residential area was established a mile or more away from the only electricity and running water, so right away there were difficulties to overcome. Just about everything needed to support a comfortable human existence had to be created from scratch. The problem was that after more than ten years on the property, many people were essentially still camping. A population explosion that more than quadrupled the number of residents on The Farm had not been matched by a surge in substantial housing or other basics to support the people.

One of the best examples of this inefficiency was The Farm's water system. In 1980, only a small percentage of homes were connected to the system by means of underground water pipes. The vast majority of Farm dwellings received water each day from a delivery truck hauling a several-thousand-gallon tank. Makeshift water towers with three- or four-hundred-gallon tanks perched on top were placed uphill from each house, tent, or shack, supplying gravity-powered running water to sinks and showers.

As participants in the communal economy, the two drivers of the water truck received no salary. To maintain daily delivery of water to all the homes, the "bank lady" simply needed to come up with money to buy gas for the truck and for vehicle maintenance. In terms of dollars, this was easier than gathering the upfront capital investment required to purchase pipe to connect the entire community, with its many different neighborhoods, to the water system.

After ten years on the land, there were only two indoor toilets in the entire community. One was in the original house, a structure that had been taken over by a Farm business, the Book Publishing Company. The other was inside the community's laundry facility. Adding flush toilets to each household was impossible without a direct connection to the water system. The amount of water necessary to support a population of fifteen hundred, all using flush toilets on a daily basis, was way beyond our capacity.

Outhouses were the norm at every home and community building. Outhouses are not inherently bad, but in communal living situations with thirty or forty people to a household, diseases, infections, intestinal parasites, and bacteria, such as *E. coli*, shigella, and giardia, were easily passed around and difficult to eliminate. Flush toilets, while not the best solution from an ecological point of view in terms of water usage or stream pollution, do provide a much more sanitary way of dealing with human waste. But lack of water and funds meant that installing flush toilets at every home was not a possibility.

Homes were also without standard electricity. The idea, of course, was that all homes would eventually be equipped with solar panels that would provide electrical power. Unfortunately, in the early 1980s the cost of solar was exorbitant. Kerosene lamps were still in place here and there, but after a few fires resulting from kerosene use, most homes had lighting provided by direct current run off car batteries, even if some residents had to haul batteries every few days to a plug-in charger on The Farm.

To say that Farm homes were without power is not completely true; they simply did not have conventional electricity. By this period the woods were filled with a tangled spaghetti of salvaged copper-coated steel phone wire that ran to a central location and connected to the standard electrical power grid, a service that became known as the "trickle charge system." Steel is an inefficient conductor of electricity because it offers so much resistance to electric current. On The Farm, when 110 volts of standard electric power was fed into a steel wire about a mile long, by the time it reached the end of the line, there was only about thirteen to fifteen volts.

After converting this to direct current, also known as DC, it provided just enough electricity to charge a car battery. The rest of the energy was lost, given off as heat generated overcoming the resistance of the steel.

Taillights and bulbs pulled from junked cars and trucks provided dim but adequate lighting, much brighter and safer than kerosene. The DC system also provided power for car stereo sound systems and small, portable black-and-white TVs, regarded as luxuries in the early days on The Farm.

Outside a tent house, a person pedals a bicycle to charge a car battery for interior lighting.

In the late 1970s, a local independent phone company upgrading their hardware at switching centers around the county offered to let The Farm scrap and salvage the old equipment. This included backup power systems and banks of batteries that were two feet high by eight feet across. These power cells had massive storage capacity and were seen as the perfect complement to the solar-powered systems that everyone hoped would be just around the corner on The Farm. In the meantime the battery banks could be energized by the trickle charge system.

Virtually every large household on The Farm was then outfitted with a set of the large battery banks. Had solar panels for every home been even a remote possibility, this arrangement would have been a step in that direction. In reality the trickle charge system was a glaring example of expedient inefficiency that did not meet the needs of a population.

One of the biggest downsides to the inadequate electricity was that it didn't supply enough energy to power refrigerators, which are appliances that modern Western society tends to take for granted. This put a strain on homemakers facing the task of preparing fresh food every day for thirty or forty people. The cooks at home had to make do without being able to rely on leftovers or daily staples like milk and tofu. Although winter brought its own struggles, such as the added work of maintaining fires for warmth and living in an environment with an abundance of mud, at least during the cold months food could be stored outside on the porch. However, life in the South means winters are short, and relying on cool outside temperatures works for only a few months at best.

The lack of power also meant our homes did not have washers or dryers. Imagine taking care of a dozen kids, half of them in diapers, and the nearest laundry is a mile or two away and you don't own a car. The Farm had its own laundry, but this was shared by twelve hundred or more people whose dirty clothing included diapers from hundreds of babies. The laundry ran twenty-four hours a day. Procuring an ideal time slot to do laundry and a good place in line became an art, and those who managed this well were respected for their skill. On top of that, with limited or no access to a vehicle, it was a challenge just to get a household's laundry delivered.

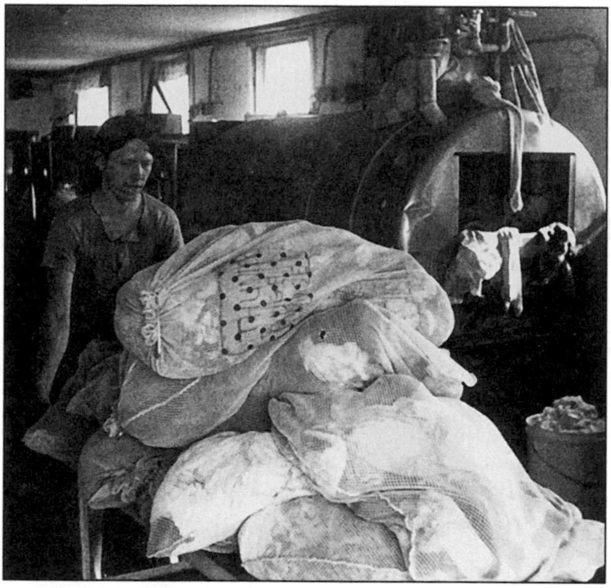

The Bronto was an industrial washing machine that did laundry in bulk, a much-appreciated service.

To help with this burden, The Laundry Crew installed a huge used industrial washing machine, manufactured to service hospitals or motels, called The Bronto. Clothes were placed in a mesh bag and washed in bulk with twenty or so other bags. Forget about separating colors and whites. After a few loads everything turned a similar dull color, but it was a much-appreciated service. Laundry bags were tagged with the name of each household and family and after being run through the system were placed on a pallet under a shed roof for pickup. The laundry was spun but still needed to be hung on a clothesline to dry. It was important to check each day to see whether a household's laundry had made it through that day's loads. Miss a day or two and the damp clothing could quickly mildew in Tennessee's intense heat and humidity.

Drying the laundry was just one more challenge. It's said that the clothesline is the original solar dryer, so it stands to reason that when the sun goes down, nothing gets dry. Tennessee's humidity meant clothes had to be brought in every night, even if they weren't completely dry. Unless this was done, the heavy dew would simply soak them again. Rain showers in Tennessee can be frequent and arrive unexpectedly during most months of the year. This became a problem when many people were away at work and the folks left at home were caring for a dozen kids and rushing to cook the evening meal before the return of a big household of hungry hippies. Most homes were deep in the woods, where sun was a limited commodity. In winter it could rain five days or more in a row. The constant sight of clothing hanging on lines inside the living area, near the woodstove, simply added to the feeling that we were living in poverty.

Although The Farming Crew made tremendous strides toward growing enough food to support the community, it could not keep up with the expanding population. Diet was very much tied to the seasons, with vegetables only available during certain times of the year. A valiant effort was put into canning and freezing for winter, but despite countless hours of labor invested, the sum of stored foods fell far short of the demand.

All food was rationed and kept to the basics. Staples that had to be purchased, including oil, sugar, and toilet paper, were distributed in carefully calculated amounts. Households were given just enough to last from week to week. Only pregnant women and kids deemed exceptionally skinny received "special" foods, such as peanut butter and bananas. Everyone accepted that things would be rough in the beginning. But as the young hippies made the shift from idealistic youths to parents responsible for the well-being of their own children, they began to see that it wasn't healthy or fair for the kids to endure a poor diet simply because their parents didn't have it together.

The Decline

Every single aspect of Farm life was affected by the financial strain. Yet in the midst of the sacrifice being made by all the members of the community, Stephen felt a calling to go on a speaking tour of Europe. Cash desperately needed at home went to cover travel expenses for Stephen and The Farm's band, along with a sizable entourage of family, public relations people, and support staff. While The Farm typically benefited from musical and speaking tours in the states because they attracted new members who contributed vehicles and cash to the community, it was unclear what might be gained by a trip abroad.

This was one of the more obvious examples that The Farm was being governed by an "abbot of the monastery" or a charismatic leader, what some might call a benevolent dictator. Many felt the community should close its doors to new members until the financial crisis was stabilized and our infrastructure was upgraded to satisfy the needs of the current population. Although this step had been taken numerous times during The Farm's early history, Stephen now opposed this. More and more, we began to feel that Stephen was not in touch with the struggles of ordinary Farm families. Our patience for continuing to live in a perpetual state of self-induced poverty was growing thin.

The disillusionment taking place on The Farm started to become obvious in 1982, when we could see that the population was no longer expanding and had instead begun to decline. The departures started as a slow trickle and grew into a wave as dozens and then hundreds of people moved off The Farm. By the fall of 1983, the community's population had dwindled to seven hundred.

The situation was starting to get desperate. The first oil crisis of the early 1980s had hit and gas prices tripled, from fifty cents to a dollar and a half a gallon. This put the squeeze on the construction industry, which had been the primary income supporting the community for many years. With the diminished income from The Construction Crew, only about $6,000 was coming into the community each week, but our weekly expenses were closer to $10,000.

The Task Force was established to address the situation. Its members included people who were taking on management roles at various levels in the community's organization. Their goal was to bring income into the community. It was no longer possible, as had been done in the early 1970s, to dispatch vanloads of young hippies to work for Manpower and at day labor jobs in Nashville. In desperation, The Task Force decided we would take on large-scale contracts to plant trees, and they began drafting teams of people to send out to the work sites. The only people who were exempt from this conscription were those who were already working at outside jobs that produced income and those who were employed by a community business that was supposed to be generating cash. People with large families of four or five kids really felt the strain when one mate was sent away for a month at a time. The conditions at the work sites were rough. It was often hot, and the terrain ranged from steep hillsides to swamps. A few people were able to push themselves hard and make a day rate of $100 to $150 by planting thousands of trees, but most were unable to maintain that pace. As a result, the money earned from this project was nowhere near what we needed. Overall, this approach to our financial problems felt like a step backward. It didn't take long before it became abundantly clear that tree-planting brigades were not going to be the solution to The Farm's financial problems.

The Farm was maturing along with its members, as the majority of members were moving from their twenties into their thirties, and many now had families to care for. It was time to get real. We were no longer interested in living on the edge. The thrilling roller-coaster ride of the last ten years had lost its appeal, and no one had any idea what was coming next.

As the members of The Task Force scrambled to understand what was going on, they undertook a financial assessment of the community. They discovered that each of the many different entities working within The Farm—the numerous small startup businesses, The Farming Crew, The Farm Clinic, The Farm Store, and many more—had opened individual checking accounts at local banks. Some had taken out loans, applied for credit, racked up bills—and no overriding entity on The Farm had been aware of the total amount of money that had been borrowed. When The Farm's bookkeepers finally accumulated all the information and added all the figures together, they discovered that the community was in debt to the tune of at least half a million dollars. Some say the figure was closer to one million dollars. The amount of money we owed seemed insurmountable.

Some of the largest chunks of debt were medical bills. Of course we didn't have health insurance. Not only was The Farm philosophically opposed to the idea of health insurance, but quite simply, living under a vow of poverty, there was no way we could afford it. The Farm's general clinic and medical staff excelled at primary care. But we weren't equipped to handle more specialized care, and we didn't have the funds to send our residents for off-site medical services. Anyone with a problem that would cost us money was put on a waiting list. Hernia operations could be postponed indefinitely. Why buy new glasses when old ones could be fixed with duct tape and glue?

By the early 1980s, The Farm's credit at local hospitals had run out and large debts from past medical services loomed menacingly, which meant hospital stays were for emergencies only. Still, in a community as large as ours, it was not unusual for serious emergencies to occur that warranted the services and expert care that only a hospital could supply. For example, in the early years, one fellow, who had taken on work as an arborist trimming trees in a nearby town, had a bad fall and landed on a chainsaw while it was running. He was hospitalized for several months while he recovered from his injuries.

Many people came to The Farm only to utilize the services of The Midwives, leaving after the delivery of their child. Occasionally there would be an emergency and transport to a nearby hospital was required. In such cases it was The Farm that got the bill, not the family with the baby.

As a matter of pride and out of commitment to our ideals, not to mention out of fairness to the people of our county and state, members of The Farm did not take welfare and did not apply for government assistance, even though our low incomes qualified us for help. This went on year after year, even as one emergency after another added up to more and more debt for the community.

Eventually it became impossible for us to pay our creditors. All the people extending credit and all the bill collectors knew that The Farm owned a big piece of land, which was our collateral. In this, our time of financial trouble, instead of extending us assistance, as the hospitals would for other Tennesseans living below the poverty line, our creditors took the approach of regarding each individual from The Farm as a large landowner, and we were charged full price for all services and treatments we received.

Finally the unthinkable happened. One of the largest hospitals in Nashville put a lien against the land.

Something had to be done, and fast. The Task Force, now formed into a true board of directors, saw no other way out.

Top: Elders introduction. Bottom: The Farm Band.

NINE

The Changeover

Although the date of The Changeover was in October 1983, this was actually a process that took place over the course of several years, punctuated by the key events that led to the breakdown of the established order and triggered shifts in Farm agreements. Marked by the end of common economic interdependence and shared income, The Changeover was also the formal dissolution of Stephen's reign. No longer could he and his family set policy or make financial decisions that affected the entire community. As time wore on, we had come to see Stephen differently. He seemed less like a divinely inspired, spiritual teacher; it had become evident that he was simply a man—a good man, but one who had ego issues that were the obvious result of too much power.

The Changeover was a dramatic shift for everyone involved in The Farm. Hundreds panicked and made a hasty exit, scattering to all corners of the country. Their security shaken, more than a few found themselves starting from scratch, with nothing to show for their efforts over the previous decade. It was as if that time had vanished into thin air. When the dust settled, a core group of about 100 adults and their 150 children remained on the land. Their resolve to save The Farm from bankruptcy and dissolution, and to maintain the integrity of the land in its entirety, shaped the foundation of the community as it exists today.

The End of the Beginning

The decision was made and a meeting was called. The Community Center was packed. It seemed like everyone was there. We all knew that something big was about to go down, but no one was quite sure what was going to happen. The board of directors sat at the front of the room. One of the board members stood up and announced that our communal economy and interdependence was over. That was it.

From that day forward, every individual and every family would be responsible for their own personal expenses—food, medical care, transportation, clothing—all the things most families in the world have to cover for themselves. But that wasn't all. Next, we were told that every person or couple would be expected to pay weekly or monthly for their portion of the community's operating expenses. Services would be cut to a bare minimum, but that wouldn't happen until a thorough cost analysis had been done of all the services The Farm provided its members. The result of that study, we were told, would be made public and all members would have a vote to approve each item and expense line in the budget, thereby placing the final reckoning in the hands of the people. In addition, each person was expected to pay monthly an equal amount toward our collective debt.

In one fell swoop, with the exception of the Book Publishing Company, which was to continue to be owned by the community, all the small businesses and enterprises on The Farm were privatized. The new policy put ownership of these entities into the hands of the principal managers, and the rest of the workers became employees who were to be paid a salary.

Nearly every aspect of our lives was about to change. The people who had the easiest time were those with skills or employment that was already part of a cash-flow system. Carpenters, painters, and others in the construction trades saw an immediate improvement in their way of life, because they started receiving paychecks that previously had been turned over to the community's central banking system. Some of the other small businesses were able to make the transition. Pay was low at first, perhaps even below minimum wage. With a forced focus to meet overhead costs and to pay actual wages to employees, several of the small businesses became viable companies over the course of the next few years.

Some enterprises did not survive. Fresh bread from The Farm's bakery was delicious but a luxury. With the majority of people starting from scratch and needing to find a job, buy a car, and spend money on so many other necessities, it would be a while before most people could afford, and the community's internal economy would be able to support, such extras.

To Stay or Not to Stay

As the news started to sink in about how the community would now operate, we all were in shock, and a pervasive numbness spread among those left on The Farm. Many people made plans to leave as soon as possible. While it was the financial situation that served as the catalyst instigating The Changeover, for many people it was the end of the dream, the mass disillusionment, that had as much or more to do with their decision to leave the community. If we were not all in it together, and it was going to be the proverbial every man for himself, then what was the point of staying? We who had been so sure of ourselves, the hippie visionaries who were going to change the world, had failed. It was a crushing blow to our egos, and the air was thick with sadness and depression.

Things had fallen too far for a pep talk from Stephen to pull us out of this one. His bubble had burst. Stephen no longer had the power or the energy to rally our vision, and as the symbol of and channel for our faith and trust in the universe, his role as a spiritual teacher disappeared like smoke floating through the air.

The community felt like a ghost town. Where once had been a bustling, thriving town, there was now only quiet and a stillness in the air. Abandoned, empty buildings stood here and there on the property. Without money for repairs and maintenance, even a few well-constructed buildings developed roof leaks and rotted to the point of collapse. Scattered throughout the property were dilapidated buildings surrounded by piles of trash and assorted junk. Of course, dozens of substandard shacks and the remains of tents needed to go. Each one was another site in need of demolition and removal. In more than a few ways, the people who chose to stay felt like the cleanup crew after Woodstock.

With each departing family, those who remained drew closer. We looked each other in the eye and said, "I'm staying. Are you staying?" For some it was a source of pride, a refusal to return to their parents, for doing so would be an admission that the whole hippie experiment had been nothing more than youthful folly, and that it was finally time to grow up, get a real job, and return to the American mainstream.

Leaving The Farm also often meant leaving a rural lifestyle. Having grown attached to the peace, serenity, and beauty of a life surrounded by nature, those who stayed felt a strong desire to buffer their children from the world of shopping malls and middle-class mediocrity.

Ultimately it came down to housing and work. With so many people exiting, each house that had served as a giant commune saw its population shrink until just one family remained, and it became their own single-family home. But there were only so many suitable structures. We dismantled the interiors of these group houses, which had been split up to make micro-bedrooms for all the former residents. Now families could have space to stretch out. As the kids grew older, it became apparent to us that, ideally, they should each have their own room. As we reconfigured the living space for comfort, the huge houses no longer seemed so big.

Abandoned shacks and tents rotted away, which was just as well because the community could only sustain the people who had a halfway decent place to live. Virtually all houses still had at least a few openings covered with stapled plastic where windows should be and had outhouses instead of toilets. Most houses still lacked electricity, and very few had exterior siding. And there was a long list of other things that needed to be repaired or improved for each and every home. Fortunately, though, the structures that remained were solid enough to get by.

Stephen Stays

Like everyone else, Stephen and Ina May Gaskin had to decide whether to stay or leave the community. Their situation was really not that different from the rest of ours. Their house was a converted army tent and needed a tremendous amount of work. Although Stephen and Ina May had become accustomed to the perks of power, it didn't mean they were corrupt. Stephen hadn't been siphoning off The Farm's money into a secret bank account. They were as broke as everyone else. Certainly, running home to Mom and Dad for help to make a new start was not an option for them. In many ways, probably the easiest thing for them to do was to simply stay put, retreat into the solitude of the Tennessee woods, and take some time to reassess their lives.

For the people who remained in the community immediately after The Changeover, the Gaskins had little relevance. Everyone was too caught up in just surviving and taking care of their own families. For quite a while it felt as though Stephen was harboring some resentment, which wasn't surprising. After being the center of attention and idolized for so many years, he had to find it shocking to be pushed aside and disregarded. We got a sense of what he was feeling when he would occasionally refer to the board members who instigated The Changeover as "closeted Republicans." It was easy to see how he would feel burned and burned out after giving so much of himself to the founding of the community.

Some people still looked up to Stephen and Ina May as leaders, but the Gaskins were on equal footing with everyone else—one man (or woman), one vote. In the years following The Changeover, Ina May ran for and was elected to the board of directors. Stephen was chosen for a position on the membership committee. It was a dramatic shift from Stephen's previous role, a change that actually made him seem more like part of the community.

Help from Outer Space

You could say I was one of the lucky ones. After returning from Guatemala, I began working with The Radio Crew's new startup company that was assembling and manufacturing Geiger counters. The business was struggling to get off the ground, and I grew frustrated. My attention was drawn to a research project being developed by two other guys on the crew, one of whom had mentored me back in the mid-1970s, when we both worked at a Farm-owned CB radio store in town. He had written Book Publishing Company's most successful title to date, *The Big Dummy's Guide to CB Radio.* Now he was doing research for a new book about an innovative technology that harvested television signals beamed from outer space: the satellite dish.

For most of us, the '80s was a time to focus on raising our families.

A huge parabolic antenna was set up in the field next to several old house trailers, where The Radio Crew and its new electronics business was based. The antenna was connected to a homemade receiver and TV, and the results of this setup were astounding. I could not believe my eyes. Suddenly blaring from the TV were channels like CNN, HBO, and a new network called MTV. I knew immediately that this was something people would buy.

We hauled the satellite dish up on the back of a small trailer pulled by a pickup truck, and rented a booth at the local county fair where we showed folks what it could do. There was a lot of interest, and a steady stream of people came by the booth to watch us flip through the channels on our receiver. A guy from one of the town's radio stations came up and told me they needed a dish, but they required a system more complicated than the ones being sold to pick up TV channels. I told him, "No problem. We can do that."

Actually I had no idea what was involved, but I got on the phone and started calling until I found an equipment distributor who said he could walk me through the setup and sell me everything I needed. I was in business!

Within a couple of months I had sold a home satellite system to a guy who owned several auto parts stores and a complex, commercial, multi-channel system to the local Holiday Inn. We placed ads in several newspapers and sales went wild. The new satellite business was on fire, and it became a cash cow for the community. Suddenly I was managing about fifteen guys and dispatching crews all around the state. Unfortunately, only a few of the staff had any technical or electronic expertise. There was plenty of grunt labor involved for each installation, but even that could be flubbed up by people who were not used to working for living, and were out of touch with professional standards and the expectations of wealthy suburbanites.

This new direction in my life called for a different type of personal sacrifice. My day started at six a.m., and I was usually not home until after nine or ten p.m., six days a week. I barely saw my family. My tendency to be a workaholic advanced to a new level.

The satellite business had been up and running for two years before we were all hit by The Changeover. Overnight, the company went from a community business to my personal business. At the same time, a loan that had been taken out to bankroll our new startup became my personal debt, around $7,000. Still, unlike so many who had no idea what they were going to do, I was at the reins of a thriving business.

The reality of The Changeover meant that instead of handing over my company's profit to the community's central bank, I had to start paying each person who worked for me. This forced me to consider the value and efficiency of each person on the crew at a time when cash flow was tight. Just a few months after The Changeover, at Christmastime, I had to lay off a lot of people. It was not fun.

To help supplement my income, I started writing for magazines related to satellite television. After a few years, when the satellite TV fad started to fade, one of the magazines changed its focus to a new consumer phenomenon: the video camera, also called the camcorder. I went out and bought one, and I started writing about making videos of my kids and how to do basic video editing. I also began reviewing new camcorders.

In looking for things to write about, I saw that other people were videotaping weddings and coming up with various ways to make money using video, and I started wondering if this was something I should try. My first job was for The Farm Building Company, which had a contract with Tennessee Valley Authority (TVA) to reconstruct an old log cabin next to one of the dams that generated electricity down in Mississippi. The job was to document the entire construction project with video and photographs. The work went on for several months.

By the end of the decade I was out of the satellite TV business altogether, dividing my time between writing for magazines and running my new video production company. My decision to stay on The Farm had a lot to do with my ability to adapt and change, as I figured out new ways to earn a living in sync with the changing times.

Exploring Freedom

The rebellion against authority was not just directed at Stephen as a central power figure, but also, in many ways, it was directed against the community itself. A number of rules and regulations had developed on The Farm over the years, and these too represented a form of authority. Although there had been a conscious effort to avoid the trappings of ritual and religious dogma, "agreements" held by the community that gave it structure and definition became their own set of rules. We accepted these as symbols of our commitment to work for the greater good of humanity.

These agreements not only defined us but also confined us, and it was in this area that we made our initial steps to assert our individualism. Some of the first agreements to break down during The Changeover had to do with personal appearance. Under the tenets of the "old" Farm, no one in the community—including men, women, and children—cut their hair, as haircutting was viewed as indulging vanity and ego. The idea was that time spent looking in a mirror shouldn't exceed what was necessary to ensure neat grooming and cleanliness. Each person's appearance was deemed "natural," as given to them by God or by life itself.

However, long hair could become problematic for young boys when they went outside the community. Often, well-meaning locals assumed they were girls, and kids their own age made fun of them. Stephen had always espoused the motto "Question authority." In the days leading up to The Changeover, a few brave individuals tested the waters by cutting their hair. Some women began to wear bras and apply a little makeup, both acts that had been taboo on The Farm. The unity of The Farm was beginning to dissolve. But demonstrating that we could make decisions as individuals was an expression of our liberation; we were no longer confined to definitions prescribed within the "cult."

Another rule was a ban on jewelry. Stephen had stated that it was immoral for someone to wear items whose value could feed the children of a starving village, and in our hearts this sentiment rang true. Jewelry was also seen as an expression of vanity and ego, at least in the early days on The Farm. After a few years, this prohibition loosened up and people were allowed to decorate jackets and other clothing with beadwork and embroidery, but an unstated peer pressure kept us from wearing "extras," such as necklaces, rings, earrings, and other decorations. While there wasn't a great rush to purchase diamond rings after The Changeover (who had that kind of money anyway?), gold wedding bands became acceptable, and pretty soon wearing jewelry became a nonissue.

As The Farm drifted more toward the mainstream center, young brides of the second generation were likely to receive diamond engagement rings. Earrings became popular, and wearing any sort of jewelry became simply a personal preference. Now, self-expression has been pushed to even greater extremes, as Western culture has changed to accept tattoos and body piercings as the new normal.

The issue of alcohol was a bit more complicated. The Farm was founded by spiritual seekers on a search for higher consciousness, and it was fairly obvious to us that drinking an excess of alcohol makes you stupid. People often make bad decisions when under the influence of alcohol, such as getting behind the wheel of an automobile when they're inebriated or hooking up with someone else's partner, which is often a catalyst for a drunken brawl. Clearly, the early Farm benefited a great deal from its no-alcohol policy, which helped set the tone for the community.

As members of the community grew older, moving into their thirties and early forties, they began to feel that not being allowed to have a cold beer after a hot, hard day's work was not only conservative but also somewhat archaic. Having a glass of wine with dinner was something millions of people did without ruining their lives. Were we not responsible grown-ups capable of making that decision for ourselves without the community setting rules for us? Even an occasional round of mixed drinks could help loosen things up and make a party a lot livelier.

In the period leading up to and just after The Changeover, breaking the rules became a forbidden but tempting fruit, and alcohol would sometimes appear at private parties. Of course the word quickly got out, and more people began to question why they were still toeing the line, why they weren't getting in on the action. Yes, you could have a beer or a glass of wine and still be a spiritual person, your same good self. It would be a number of years before alcohol's dark side would rear its ugly head.

Divorce

Another area of personal freedom that opened up in the post-Changeover years was divorce. Divorce was taboo on the early Farm, because it was seen as an inability to work things out or to make the personal changes necessary to grow as a person and as a suitable marriage partner. The close quarters of communal living arrangements combined with truth telling and calling people out on their ego trips did in fact help many couples stay together. However, by the late '70s, even Stephen and Ina May had to admit that some marriages were not working out and it would be better for both people in the relationship to call it quits.

In the immediate years after The Changeover, with members no longer under this type of intense scrutiny or forced to suppress their true feelings to save face, there was an abrupt wave of people breaking up. Perhaps some had been caught up in the marriage fever of the early Farm and had not taken the time to get to know each other to discover whether they were truly compatible. Others had simply drifted apart, as couples often do. The crumbling of marriages, once heralded as an example of our communal strength, was yet another representation of the rifts within the community. These splits, along with the pain and the freedom that attended them, were in fact symbolic of the stress and strain we'd all lived under and from which we were emerging. In the decades following The Changeover, divorce returned to the same status it has everywhere, an unfortunate fact of life.

If divorce on The Farm is in any way different from that in the greater society, it is the degree to which couples are able to set aside their differences and remain friends. When it works, the love that originally brought two people together returns as mutual affection, underscored by their bond of shared children and shared ideals. When enough time has passed to heal the raw hurt, friendship and respect reappear, visibly expressed through both social and personal interaction as members of a greater community.

Alternative Lifestyles and Relationships

Another area of Farm life that opened up in the era of newfound freedom had to do with relationships and sexual orientation. Very early on, it was recognized that women often bore the brunt of the so-called sexual revolution, or free love, associated with the hippie movement. They were often left to raise children on their own when men, that is to say fathers, did not take responsibility for their actions. When this was brought to Stephen's attention on the bus Caravan, he issued a decree: "If you're sleeping together, you are engaged. If you're pregnant, you are married. Nobody walks away from a baby."

The Farm's spiritual philosophy emphasized the power of life force energy, and like the Catholic Church, its interpretation included a prohibition on birth control pills and other forms of contraception. Living under this reality meant that couples wishing to have sex felt strong peer pressure to get married. Because most of those coming to The Farm were in their twenties and early thirties, they were at the phase of life when people are ready to begin settling down and start a family. At times it seemed as if Stephen was performing marriage ceremonies almost every Sunday, sometimes two, three, even as many as six at a time. Consequently there was a strong emphasis on family, the traditional nuclear family, that was underscored by the community's acknowledgment that birth was a sacrament and its midwives were elders of The Farm Church.

As in most of America in the 1970s, during those early years on The Farm, gays and lesbians stayed in the closet. Caught up in the energy of The Farm and its strong emphasis on family, many found opposite-sex partners, married, and had children. In 1981, after he returned from a speaking tour of California, Stephen announced that he had gained a better understanding and an acceptance of the gay lifestyle, but it wasn't until the social restructuring leading up to The Changeover that any member of the community felt brave enough to come out. This declaration of sexual preference at times coincided with a person's departure from the community. Often word would filter back to those remaining in Tennessee that, sometime after leaving, a former member had announced his or her true sexual orientation, which included not just being gay or lesbian but also transgender. It was understandable that undergoing such a major personal transformation would coincide with starting over in a new life.

After The Changeover, a person's sexual orientation became a nonissue in the community, especially with so much attention going to personal economic survival. Over time, several members came out of the closet. Other gay members moved back to the community, feeling that the strong sense of family was now open to all.

Private Property

The shift from commune to collective in many ways can be defined by the change in attitude by the community about private property. In The Farm's communal phase, no one held personal money. All income was turned over to the community's central bank. For the most part, this meant that the ownership of "things" was limited to items people had owned before they joined the community and to gifts they received from their families while living on The Farm. Certain items, including basic tools, could be owned, but large or expensive tools became the property of the community. Probably the most valuable personal item an individual might own was a musical instrument, and this was typically something that had been a personal possession before arrival.

Cameras fell into a gray area. A cheap point-and-shoot camera was something that could be owned, but there was no money in the community's budget for purchasing film or developing personal snapshots. Parents or grandparents off The Farm might purchase a camera for their kid living on The Farm in order to receive pictures of their grandchildren. That's the way it worked for us. Deborah's parents gave us a camera and would send us film, and then we would mail it back to them to get it developed. Often new members arriving with more expensive 35 mm film cameras were expected to turn them into the community's Photography Crew. Some were able to get around this by joining The Photography Crew, thereby maintaining possession of their cameras because they used them in service to the community.

One of the most expensive items typically owned by an individual in mainstream society is a car or truck. During the communal period, people who arrived at The Farm with a vehicle were expected to turn it over to the community Motor Pool once they became members. The mechanics at The Motor Pool maintained the fleet to the best of their abilities, and vehicles were distributed by need. Most work crews required a vehicle to perform their job or service, especially those working outside The Farm. Construction crews needed vans and trucks. So did The Farming Crew. The Farm Midwives were on call twenty-four hours a day to respond to women delivering babies, and there were times when they had to get somewhere fast. Each active midwife received a vehicle, which may or may not have been licensed and tagged to drive outside the community. Some people on The Farm had the job of making weekly runs to town to purchase food and other necessities. The community's bankers went into town to make deposits. The Book Publishing Company would usually have a vehicle for any number of reasons, from driving to nearby Columbia to taking longer trips to Nashville to making sales runs across the country.

For the most part, the general members of The Farm got around on foot or by bicycle. However, in order for a large communal household of thirty to forty people to be able to manage all its needs, it was best if at least one person in the mix had access to a vehicle. This enabled the household to shuttle massive loads of dirty clothes up to the community's central laundry, transport food and dry goods from The Farm Store, and deal with a host of other chores that were more easily done by car or truck. The only alternative was to carry laundry or foodstuffs by hand, pull it in a wagon or wheelbarrow, or drag it behind a bike outfitted with a cart. Occasionally a household might even have its own vehicle—typically one that was old and deemed unsuitable for a crew—but this was most likely to be the case if a member of the household also just happened to work in The Motor Pool.

Ideally, The Motor Pool maintained a small fleet of vehicles that could be dispatched to individuals for personal needs. For example, during most of the early years on The Farm, cars were used once a week to take people off-site to visit a doctor or dentist. Occasionally someone might be allowed to get a pair of glasses or new shoes, and a vehicle would be needed for a trip off The Farm. Town runs were coordinated so that several people would drive in together, making the rounds to each person's stop.

Most vehicles turned over to the community by new members were old to begin with, and the rough, dusty dirt roads of The Farm were especially hard on vehicles. Without much money for parts and maintenance, just keeping a few cars roadworthy was a challenge for The Motor Pool.

As you might expect, there were other ways of working the system to get around the rules. After Deborah and I returned from Guatemala, our families gave us bus money so we could visit them. When considering everything—the cost of bus fare, the safety of bus travel with small children, and the small hassle of picking us all up at the bus station—this seemed to be a less-than-desirable way for us to visit our families, who lived about six hours north of The Farm. My parents came up with a solution: They gave us an old work van from their business, one that they were no longer using. To get around the need to turn it over to The Farm Motor Pool, when we returned to The Farm, we set the empty van up as a bedroom for a Farm teenager who was living at our household, away from his parents. About twice a year, when we would make a trip to visit our folks, the teen would move out of the van and sleep in our bedroom inside the main house. He'd move back into the van when we got back. That way we were not using the van as our own personal vehicle on The Farm, which would have given us a luxury or privilege other people didn't have.

It didn't hurt that the van was parked at the last house at the end of a long road, where it was essentially kept out of sight. Of course eventually the word got out. One day the fellow functioning as the community manager came up and asked me to turn in the van so it could be used by one of the off-site work crews. I stood my ground, explaining that the van did not belong to me; it was owned by my folks and they were just letting us use it. The guy really could not force me to turn it over, and anyway it was being used as housing, my ace in the hole. It turned out to be a good thing that I did not turn the van over to The Farm, because shortly after The Changeover my folks asked for it back.

The ability to own a vehicle was one of the biggest initial shifts of The Changeover. With each person or family now responsible for their own food, health care, and employment, acquiring a vehicle was a top priority. Of course this was no small task, especially for those leaving positions from within The Farm's now defunct services and striking out on their own for the first time. How do you get a job without a car? How do you buy a car if you don't have any money? How do you save money for a car when you are working for minimum wage to support a family? For most of us, the early years of The Changeover were an uphill struggle.

Just the simple step of getting a car was a move toward freedom. With a car, you could drive to town and buy groceries, take your kids to a movie, make trips to visit the family, all without going through a central authority for permission. Even people living in abject poverty in the rest of the country had a car. We were on our way up.

Housing

There is no question that inadequate housing was a source of frustration for just about everyone on the early Farm. On the post-Changeover Farm, it could also be said that housing came to define who would stay and who would leave. There was no attempt to come up with any system to dole out the living quarters based on fairness or need. It was more like a game of musical chairs; it all depended on where you were living when the music stopped. If, after The Changeover, you were stuck inside a leaky tent, and with no real way to support your family, the community's future could appear pretty bleak.

The large communal households emptied out as person after person and couple after couple gave up on The Farm and moved away. Finally, only a single family would remain in a home and they became its "owners." While some folks came into possession of reasonably solid, multistory, multibedroom dwellings that seemed to us like minimansions, others found themselves in dilapidated shacks. That's just the way it was.

About a year or so before The Changeover, Deborah and I had left one of the large households to move into a school bus for some peace and quiet with just our family. The bus served as our family bedroom. It was parked a couple of hundred feet from a small shack on the side of a hill. The shack had a kitchen, bathroom (tub and sink), a small living room, and an upper floor that had three bedrooms—one for each of the other two couples and one that their kids shared. After The Changeover, one of the couples left and we moved inside. Eventually it was just our family living there.

The shack, called Huckstones, didn't have a proper foundation and was built too close to the ground. There had been no thought in the design about proper drainage, and water rushing down the hillside ran under the floor, causing it to warp and buckle. Some of the windows were just openings covered by plastic, and even those with glass panes were leaky, letting in lots of cold air. It was quite frigid in the wintertime, and despite the fire in our woodstove downstairs, the only warm spot for us and the kids was in our upstairs bedroom, where we huddled under the covers.

Because so many people were leaving after The Changeover, those who remained sometimes had the opportunity to move into new housing that had opened up. Another couple, good friends from The Green River Farm, came into possession of a large log cabin home that had been converted into a duplex. When a family left and one side of the duplex opened up, our friends offered it to us. It was a lucky break.

Of course, like many of the homes from the early Farm, the cabin needed a lot of work. As two families sharing a duplex, in a very real way we continued to live as a communal household. We had separate kitchens and some private quarters, but we shared other space and also split the cost of improvements to the cabin. Together, over those first few years, we put on a new roof, installed all new windows, added exterior siding on the second floor, installed a toilet, connected a new electrical service, built a chimney, set up a wood-fired central heating system, and on and on. Everyone who inherited one of the homes built during the communal period had to make similar investments.

Introspection

The remainder of the 1980s became a period of introspection for people living on The Farm, a time for each of us to focus on how we would take care of ourselves and our families. Commitment to the community was expressed by faithfully paying our share of the monthly budget. Virtually everyone was starting from scratch, buying a first car, making a home more livable. Little by little the houses went from unfinished shells to humble abodes, as we added the finishing touches that most people in this country take for granted.

Because of its reputation, The Farm still had a steady flow of visitors, but what had once been part of the fun, showing off our community, became a burden. Most who came to check us out were disappointed not to find the legendary commune brimming with hippies, and these visitors were often critical of the changes. They wanted to see endless rows of crops, not abandoned fields lost in weeds. Farm folks began to avoid interaction. These commune tourists had no clue about the struggles that all of us who stayed were going through just to keep The Farm alive.

The same was true of the media. For the first decade of its existence, The Farm had been an easy feel-good story for journalists across the country. Everyone from *People* magazine to *60 Minutes* wanted to know what had happened to the hippies and what they were up to after San Francisco. When a glossy Tennessee magazine came in and produced a story about how we'd become a ghost town, it was evident to us that The

Farm did not need that sort of publicity. Because the community was no longer operating with a staff of public relations people promoting Stephen, there wasn't anyone on deck to interface with the press. We had no official voice to present our story about The Changeover and where we were heading now. With the hippie dream all but forgotten, Reagan in the White House, and the country shifting to the right, the media wasn't much interested in us anyway.

Still, we had each other, and though our numbers had greatly diminished, even one hundred people was enough to make for lively parties. Within the larger group, smaller circles of close friendships began to evolve. The bonds among those who stayed were perhaps even stronger than what had been possible during the peak population of the 1970s.

Although this was a period of struggle, we couldn't deny the positive shift in energy created by The Changeover. Suddenly it was okay to possess previously unaffordable commodities, such as orange juice. In our new world, we were experiencing some simple freedoms: we could take the kids for a big night out on the town and visit an all-you-can-eat salad bar.

The Changeover "officially" took place on a day early in the week, and on the following Saturday, a group of about one hundred people scraped together a few bucks, packed themselves inside any vehicle they could commandeer, and rode to Nashville to see a real live rock concert. I was among them, hunched over in the rear of a VW hatchback. The band was The Talking Heads, and there was a certain irony in the name of the tour, "Stop Making Sense." We danced our asses off, and the feeling was one of pure exhilaration.

It may be hard to believe, but only about three years after The Changeover, the majority of The Farm's debt was paid off, and before the end of the decade, the land was free and clear. The worst was over. We had survived. Now the question was "What next?"

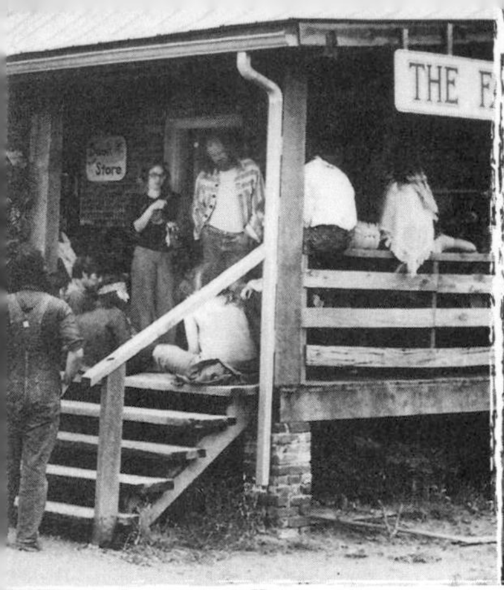

TEN

Finding New Strengths

By the time the 1990s rolled around, the dust from The Changeover had settled. The base population on The Farm had stabilized, and those who remained had settled into some method of supporting themselves and their families. The debt on the land had been paid off by the late 1980s, so the task of operating and making new improvements to the community's infrastructure could be determined through an annual assessment and approval of a budget confirmed by a democratic vote. A working system of government was in place. We'd achieved a lot in a relatively short time. Not only had we cleared our debts, but also we'd improved our living conditions and created a new version of our original dream. The image and face of The New Farm was emerging.

If the 1980s had been a period of introspection, then the 1990s was a time when the community began to lift its head and see that it still had something to offer, that it still could be a viable example of an alternative to mainstream society. One of the more subtle, but nonetheless important, accomplishments, we felt, was that The Farm had survived the tenure of Ronald Reagan. The 1980s had been marked by a direct assault on everything that might fall under the heading of counterculture values. As the nation made a hard shift to the right, expressed as rampant materialism, it cast aside many of the social programs, alternative energy initiatives, and environmental concerns of previous decades. In a way, The Farm had taken on a new role, serving as a symbol of counterculture values, offering hope and inspiration to all those who had been forced to give up their ideals.

Teenagers

Perhaps The Farm's biggest challenge of the 1990s was dealing with a population of nearly 150 teenagers, all raised to question authority and steeped in the roots of hippie freedom. Some rebelled against their parents more forcefully than others. Youth's drive for independence may simply be Mother Nature's way of getting parents to kick baby birds out of the nest. Although The Farm's adult members had shared a cultural experience and, as a group, embraced similar spiritual ideals, members of the founding generation still had their own personal histories that established their parenting styles. And this was especially brought into play when it came to the way families dealt with matters such as discipline, rules, and education—issues all parents face.

It also became abundantly clear that every child is different, born with a singular personality and disposition, yet all are molded by the times and environment during which they come of age. Families had to come to grips with this reality. Some were blessed with kids who were easy, while others were frustrated by offspring who tested the resolve and patience not just of their parents, but quite often the community as a whole.

In the cities and larger towns of our country, teenagers and young adults are able to perform some of their more irresponsible behavior away from the watchful eyes of parents and extended family. This can be one of the less acknowledged reasons kids go away to college. In a close-knit community like The Farm, few activities go unnoticed. The main hangout area for Farm teens was a bonfire pit in the center of the community, a place called the Head of the Roads. Trash cans overflowing with empty beer bottles as well as some empties from hard liquor were disturbing reminders for us of youth's fascination with alcohol and a tendency to drink that sometimes coincides with what may appear to parents as a listless lack of direction. As a community that had originally shunned alcohol but had opened up social acceptance to responsible drinking, we now had to bear witness to the excesses typical of kids coming of age elsewhere in Western culture. It was an interesting situation. Here we were, a group of hippies who had built our reputation as the physical representatives of youthful rebellion, and now we found ourselves in the role of "conservative" grown-ups. This was yet another transition for our group, and it is, no doubt, one that many families experience.

Fortunately, time does not stand still. Eventually most of the children who had been born on The Farm or had grown up there graduated from high school and either went on to college or left to explore the wider world. A good-sized handful stayed and never left. Over the years, there was a constant ebb and flow, leaving and returning. It seemed this next generation was taking longer to get settled on its own, standing in marked contrast to the exodus of young people in the 1960s and '70s, who could not wait to leave home. In the decades to follow, Farm parents were able to watch the excesses of youth fade as their kids matured, became adults, and then grew to be parents with kids of their own to worry about.

Throughout the 1990s, there was an influx of young people in their late twenties and thirties who were interested in making the The Farm their home. They tended to be the children of people from the older end of The Farm's original population, many of whom had left at the time of The Changeover. This group of young adults would return, nostalgic for the place that many still regarded as home. But without a number of friends in their age range, few from that group of returnees remained on The Farm for long. Everyone needs to feel that they have friends, people their own age to relate with. Young people also require a bit more action, a livelier social scene than what could be found on The Farm at that time. In the 1990s, The Farm's general population was still dominated by its founding generation, whose ages during this decade ranged from early forties to midfifties.

Those in their late twenties and early thirties who trickled back to The Farm during this period, seeking the life they remembered during a more robust time, would eventually get discouraged by the lack of contemporaries, and they'd move on. Before long, others would arrive to take their place, stay for a few months, and leave. We would watch it happen again and again.

Returns

The 1990s was also a time when the flow of people reversed. Instead of watching as members continued to leave, we started to see former residents who had departed during the 1980s make the decision to move back. For a significant number of this group, the allure of a more affluent life in suburban America had worn thin. Those former members who took the opportunity to visit old friends still living on The Farm began to question which lifestyle was more appealing: living in a community, surrounded by friends and in the midst of nature's beauty, or living in isolation in the city, as a full-fledged member of the rat race.

During this time, while some who joined the community were newcomers, more often than not the people who seemed to feel most comfortable and who stayed on The Farm were the returning former members. There were several reasons for this. Former members already had a circle of established friends. They also had a common history with other members of The Farm and understood the culture. This was especially important when it came to shared ownership of the land, homes, and extensive infrastructure.

Throughout the 1970s and the first decade of the early Farm, we had always held a big picnic around the Fourth of July, the day when most of America celebrated the peak of summer. As the community became more connected to Native American culture, Stephen put forward the idea that it might be more appropriate to make our party separate from the Fourth, so as not to celebrate the official confiscation of this country's land from native peoples.

After an unsuccessful raid on The Farm by authorities on July 11, 1980, when an overeager drug task force helicopter pilot mistook ragweed growing in a watermelon patch for marijuana, our summer event was christened Ragweed Day, and it became an annual festival of music, picnics, swimming, and fun. After The Changeover, a number of the musicians who remained on The Farm as members, myself included, felt it was important for the community's self-esteem to keep the summer party going, and the community supported this idea through active participation. As word spread throughout the greater tribe, now scattered around the country, the July event became an annual pilgrimage, especially among the youth who had spent their formative years on The Farm.

After a few years, it became clear that Ragweed Day had evolved into a Farm family reunion. It provided the perfect opportunity for former members to renew old ties and get a closer look at how the other half lived. With The Farm's infrastructure much improved, its residents no longer controlled by an autocracy, and dirt-poor poverty a thing of the past, the reasons most people felt compelled to leave no longer existed. Former residents who came to visit during the annual reunions would sometimes take the next step, returning to establish homes and full membership in The New Farm.

Outreach

With the community on secure footing, we began to explore new forms of outreach and interacting with society at large. For the members of

The New Farm, the goal of effecting social change was, and continues to be, expressed by following the precept of Right Livelihood—doing work that is seamless with our ideals. Farm members are free to define this guiding principle in any manner that works best for them, which is reflected through the diversity of paths they've chosen.

In the late 1980s and early 1990s, some members began to wonder if The Farm could fill a niche as host to various festivals, conferences, and gatherings that would be open to the public. It took some trial and error to find the types of events that were a good fit with the community. It was no problem bringing in one hundred midwives for a weekend, but it was a bit more challenging to manage four hundred alternative-schoolers, a crowd with kids of all ages who roamed our expansive acreage of forests and fields with joyous abandon. All things considered, we soon discovered that groups with a focus and purpose were much easier to absorb than festivalgoers intent on partying till dawn's early light.

Inspired by an annual music festival in North Carolina that a number of us had regularly attended, we decided to hold a similar festival of our own. I was one of the main organizers. For the first several years, we drew in a crowd of about three hundred, just enough to barely break even. Unfortunately, that meant that we fell far short of what we needed to make any money. Artists and craft vendors need a large crowd to make a festival worth their while, and in our case the vendors were disappointed, which made them less likely to return in successive years. After sending out mailings, putting up posters, and working hours and hours of volunteer time, it hardly seemed worth the effort.

At first, to keep the expenses down, we featured bands that were willing to play for free. Most were pretty good, but a few were downright embarrassing. Some of the festival organizers thought if the music lineup included bigger names and more professional acts, that might help draw a larger crowd. Of course this increased the overhead, especially when we hired artists with some level of national name recognition.

After about ten years, the crowd for our annual festival had grown to one thousand, still pretty small compared to major music festivals but quite an influx of people to our normally quiet community. Although we promoted our events as alcohol-free, this became impossible to enforce, which made security a more formidable issue. Another negative aspect for us were the frantic calls from parents looking for their teenagers who had run away for the weekend to be at our festival. Neighbors began to complain about the loud, thumping bass tones rattling their windows in the wee hours of the night. We had break-ins and the occasional weirdo. It all became too much.

Taken as a whole, our festivals had great vibes, great music, interesting workshops, cultural diversity, activities for kids, and a long list of other reasons why those attending loved every minute of what we had to offer. Ultimately, however, it was too much work for too little money and too many heavy liabilities. We'd given it a good try, but we had to concede that this vision of a cottage industry was not going to work.

Instead, those of us interested in this type of outreach began to shift our focus to bringing in small groups for a specific purpose, such as to learn about alternative building techniques and energy production. The Farm Midwives have been the most successful in applying this new strategy, hosting about a dozen seven-day workshops each year with a class size of fifteen to twenty students. Their classes are always filled to capacity, and often would-be students have to be put on a waiting list.

After an inspiring visit to the Findhorn community in Northern Scotland, I returned and organized our Farm Experience Weekends. Because our community is spread out over several miles and its members are engaged in their own lives, to the random visitor dropping in, the place can seem very quiet. The visitor may wonder where all the people are hiding. The Farm Experience Weekend offers a glimpse into how we live and includes a historical overview of The Farm, a tour of the community, and a chance to participate in workshops on green building, alternative education, midwifery, and other aspects of life on The Farm.

Neighbors

When the buses first arrived in Tennessee, a conscious effort was made to befriend The Farm's immediate neighbors. A few Farm folks would go out to visit neighbors up and down the lane outside our entrance, and we got to know a few farmers. During the first decade, some people from The Farm interacted with the outside world in a variety of different ways, but most of the population was cloistered inside the community and didn't mix it up that much with the locals.

During the 1980s and 1990s, most Farm residents became more deeply intertwined with all aspects of local life and the people of middle Tennessee. Our people built their homes. We worked in their hospitals and clinics. We shopped in local stores, set up bank accounts, bought insurance, had appliances repaired, joined clubs, received deliveries, and on and on. The Tennesseans got to know us. We became part of the local community and were ultimately embedded into its history and accepted for who we are and what The Farm represents.

Nonprofits

As The Farm emerged from the 1980s, it became increasingly clear that nonprofit organizations were an important tool for members of the community to use as a way to express their vision for a better world. The Farm Midwifery Center, The Farm School (as the Farm Educational Conference Center), Swan Conservation Trust (a land trust creating a nature preserve), and the Natural Rights Center, just to name a few, were either created or became more established during the decade of the 1990s. The main office of Plenty International, which had moved to California during The Changeover, came back to its home base when the director and his wife (who managed the organization's books) returned to live on The Farm. Programs like Kids to the Country, which brings children from homeless shelters and refugee centers down for weeklong stays on The Farm, have helped maintain the community's original vision of service to humanity and our goal of creating positive change in the world.

Throughout the early years on The Farm, there had always been members who experimented with alternative technologies, such as wind and solar power. In the late 1970s and during the Carter presidential years, Farm-based companies and nonprofits received a number of grants to develop innovative designs, such as solar photovoltaic concentrators and the first solar-powered electric vehicles. We demonstrated these innovations at the 1982 World's Fair in Knoxville, Tennessee.

The Ecovillage Training Center (ETC) was established by Farm member Albert Bates in the early 1990s to further those efforts and ideas, and it continues to serve as both a teaching facility and experimental laboratory. Students, educators, and innovators work together to develop new, ecologically sound energy production. Training Center apprentices learn construction methods based on using natural building materials and have the opportunity to work on a variety of projects. Students and apprentices from more than sixty countries have made their way to the ETC. Some stay for a number of years, and a few never leave, using the "back door" entrance through the Training Center as their path to full-time residency in the greater community.

The Farm School was one of the institutions hardest hit by The Changeover. As the community endeavored to reduce operating costs to the bare minimum, many members came to regard our private school as a luxury. Maintaining the school and paying the staff salaries added up to a costly commodity. In the throes of poverty and now without communal support, many families felt they could not afford to send their children to a private school, especially when public school was a free option. On the other hand, many parents in the community regarded The Farm School as a key part of the kit, a vitally important means for instilling and passing on the community's alternative values to their children.

Now forced to fend for themselves, parents and teachers, often one and the same, began working together to ensure the school's survival. Families helped keep their tuition costs low by doing work exchange, teaching classes to cover the cost of their children's attendance. Fortunately, there were also a few folks with higher incomes who did not have the time to teach but were able to pay, creating a much-needed infusion of cash. The community helped by maintaining the building, even paying the electric bill in those early years. Paid teachers and administrators worked for salaries below minimum wage because of their devotion to this educational system.

A few years after The Changeover, however, a number of parents began to question whether their children were receiving an adequate education at The Farm School. Because the teachers were also parents with whom the students had a deep familiarity, it often seemed that the kids did not give their elders much respect. Children who were self-motivated did well, but those students who needed a little more structure and discipline could easily become slackers.

Deborah and I were among those parents who wondered whether The Farm School was benefiting their children. It was hard to think about sending our kids away from the nurturing atmosphere of the community and into the white-bread squareness of public schools, but at the same time, we felt a responsibility to ensure our children had a real education to carry them forward in life.

The Lewis County public school in Hohenwald was about fifteen miles away and required an hour-long bus ride each way. The school in Summertown was just down the road a couple of miles but was in a different county, so technically our kids were not eligible. We really didn't want our kids to be stuck on a long bus ride every day. Through some finagling and the help of some sympathetic local friends, we registered our kids with a Summertown address and got them in. School officials turned a blind eye, anxious for the additional warm bodies that generated federal dollars. With a fresh haircut for our hippie son and new school clothes for our son and daughter, our children entered school with instructions to tell anyone who asked that they lived in Summertown and not to mention The Farm. Several other Farm parents figured out a workaround as well, so our kids were not alone.

Of course we didn't fool anyone. Teachers, administrators, and the other students were well aware that this new influx of students came from the hippie Farm, and our children received their first exposure to the more conservative South. It also opened our kids' eyes to the extremes of poverty right in their state. Although we felt as if we were poor on The Farm, once our kids had the chance to mingle with the variety of children at the public school, they were able to see the dirt-poor conditions and the ways many impoverished people continue to live in the rural South. Maybe we weren't so bad off after all.

We were still outsiders, but one move we made helped us break the ice and become better friends with our neighbors. We signed the Farm kids up for the local Little League. We had a bunch of adolescents who needed something to do, and there was this community ball tournament just a little ways down the road. As the word spread around, Farm parents mutually decided it would be good for the kids to participate, and we gave it a go. We joined in the fun of yelling for our team and rooting for our hitters. Some of our kids went on to be star players. We got to develop friendships with the coaches and other families. A lot of those adults were the same age we were, and because we'd all grown up in the 1960s and '70s, there were ways we could relate to each other as parents from the same generation. They could see we were a lot like them. Person after person would come up to say, "I remember y'all when the buses came in."

Some families stuck with the Summertown school, but for us the public school experiment served a purpose, and then we returned our children to The Farm School. While in public school, our kids learned how to stay in their seats, listen attentively, and do homework. After three years, when they were ready to move on to junior high and high school, we brought them back to The Farm School. They returned with a greater appreciation and understanding of what The Farm was about and much more respect for the freedom and other benefits The Farm School had to offer.

Did children attending The Farm School get an adequate education? The answer has as much to do with the child as with the school. While it remains true that self-motivated students have always done best at The Farm School, it is also a fact that The Farm School benefits children by giving them skills that include, but go beyond, academic training. The Farm School's educational advantage is its goal of helping children find the interests and strengths they naturally possess, which encourages their pursuit of learning. The vast majority of Farm School graduates go on to higher education. A fair number have received scholarships or finished at the head of their class.

As the 1990s came to an end, and children raised on The Farm grew up and left home, the community's population continued to decline. Would any of those children come back to stay? Would this be a one-shot deal, evolving into a hippie old-folks home before fading away? We could only wonder and move on with our lives.

A festival at The Farm.

ELEVEN

The New Farm

The Farm's colorful, hippie heyday is now but a distant memory. Even the great Changeover, the defining moment of The New Farm, is now decades in the past. The Farm community has not only survived but also continues as a model lifestyle for the world at large, demonstrating that humans can live together in a way that is ecological, peaceful, and viable. The collective land base remains intact, and the shared ownership of all buildings, homes, and infrastructure, combined with a robust internal economy and integration with the world at large, make The Farm today a hybrid capitalist enterprise blended with tribal-style focus on land stewardship.

As the community's original founders age and enter what is typically regarded as the retirement years, a new generation of young people is becoming more established, starting families of their own, and slowly taking over management of The Farm. To be sure, the community faces a variety of new challenges. Which values, principles, and agreements put in place by the founding members will pass on and which will be abandoned? Do those inheriting The Farm's legacy have the same internal drive to "save the world"? Do they share the sense of oneness and idealism that has held the community together through difficult times?

In many ways the financial, environmental, and social calamities facing our world today were foreseen by The Farm's founders. As the world economy struggles and comes to terms with the depletion of resources and the uncertain future of climate change, The Farm continues to be a flagship alternative-lifestyle community. It remains a beacon pointing to nontraditional options in building, energy, land management, education, and health care, and exemplifies how people can live together. At the same time, for its members, The Farm is also a lifeboat, an island oasis buffered from a world increasingly manipulated by international banks and corporations—a world in which individuals must fend for themselves.

Organization and Structure

The Farm's organizational structure and management has remained much the same over the years since The Changeover. Each person living full-time on the land is expected to contribute an equal monthly amount based on an annual budget divided by the total number of members. Visitors living on the land for more than thirty days, called "residents," as well as people who have applied to become provisional members, contribute the same amount, which helps compensate for revenue shortfall when full members have fallen ill, lost their means of employment, or for any other reason are unable to meet their monthly obligations. These additional funds can also offset cost overruns or unexpected increases in any budget category.

Businesses on The Farm are also assessed an amount to contribute to the annual budget based on the community services and infrastructure they use. For example, a business that receives regular deliveries by large trucks or schedules daily pickup services with companies such as Federal Express or UPS is expected to contribute to the cost of road maintenance.

The addition of monthly contributions by non-members and businesses on The Farm has enabled the community to maintain a budget surplus year after year. Beyond that, members with higher incomes are encouraged to pledge additional funds to support projects and services that go beyond the scope of the mandatory minimum monthly dues. This allows projects to move forward that many members would like to see implemented but can't afford, thereby increasing the benefits for all who choose to live in the community.

The majority of items in The Farm's annual budget are fixed costs, such as staff salaries, insurance fees, operating the community's water system, and trash and recycling pickup charges. In addition, this spending plan puts aside money for occasional needs, including roadside mowing and public building maintenance.

Some items on the budget—usually high-ticket items—become fixed costs for a set number of years, after they have been approved by a community vote. When the community decided to blacktop the main road, for instance, funding for this major capital improvement was accomplished by borrowing from our own savings, or development fund, and repaying the debt over a period of several years. The development fund is capitalized through the membership fee paid by individuals when they are voted into the community. In addition to funding large community projects, the development fund makes small to moderate-sized loans to community members for home-improvement projects and other personal needs.

The Farm continues to be managed by a seven-person board of directors elected through democratic vote. Board members shoulder the fiscal responsibility for all aspects of the community, including the collection of membership dues and subsequent dispersal of funds. The board manages and oversees people who work in various part-time service roles for the community, such as the administrator of the Welcome Center, the bookkeeper, and The Farm manager. As might be expected, the number and variety of responsibilities on the board's plate goes well beyond simply administering financial decisions. Virtually all aspects of life in the community are deeply intertwined. As the ultimate governing body, The Farm board is where the buck stops.

The process of integrating new members is the responsibility of the membership committee, which is also a democratically elected body. Another important function of the membership committee is to mediate disputes between members, a process that can consume a fair amount of time and energy. The membership committee also oversees and continues to make improvements to the community's bylaws.

A host of additional committees are staffed by volunteers whose job is to oversee other aspects of the community, including finance, land use, and housing, to name a few. The volunteer committees make recommendations to the board of directors and to the community. The committees are empowered to make decisions and set policy, but these can be challenged and are subject to the approval of the board as well as all community members. Each volunteer committee is chaired by a member of the board of directors, so that there is a direct line of communication with the elected management body. Committees give reports at quarterly community meetings and post announcements via a variety of community-wide media, such as the weekly e-newspaper and by email updates. Additionally, they may initiate an e-discussion group for those interested in hashing over current issues in greater detail.

Management through a democratically elected board has its pros and cons, but has generally worked for us for over thirty years. Any member who desires greater involvement in community government and decision making is welcome to run for a term. The challenge can be finding people willing to invest the time for what can be a thankless job. Anyone seeking a board position can get elected, because there's rarely competition; usually there's just one candidate for each open seat.

At the same time, one thing we have learned through the years is that there are certain people who have the personality and skills for facilitating meetings and making decisions, along with financial acuity and the ability to endure the barrage of a hundred or more opinionated community members whose tempers can flare during discussions of controversial issues. Consequently, the same people often are elected to office three or four times, but they don't always serve these terms consecutively.

This form of government creates a top-down management system, which has both positive and negative qualities. It places the burden of dealing with the minutia of community life on the shoulders of a few, which allows the greater Farm population to go on about their daily lives knowing that the bases are essentially covered. A petition system, though seldom used, was designed to provide checks and balances to board decisions. In practice, though, solutions for issues that don't have a healthy degree of community support have a way of stalling until plans satisfactory to the overwhelming majority of people are worked out. The consensus model of decision making requires 100 percent agreement and even one person can block something from moving forward. In contrast, Farm votes are generally based on a simple majority of a quorum of the members.

The exception to this is a membership vote, which requires two-thirds of the entire voting body to approve candidates for membership. Candidates who do not receive enough votes don't have to leave the community. They're given time to work on issues that may have prevented their acceptance. A negative vote simply reflects that a sufficient number of people have questions about a candidate's potential to fit in with the community. These sticking points might range from concern about a candidate's lack of participation in community activities and attendance at community meetings to worries over talk that a would-be member's behavior has rubbed various folks the wrong way. It can also mean that some voters don't feel they know the person well enough. Occasionally an individual will not receive the required number of votes because several people who would have approved were out of town. In the case of a no vote, a candidate's Farm sponsor will urge that person to examine the issues that led to rejection and to try to change things, perhaps by forging better relationships within the community.

All elections and votes generally take place over several days in order to give everyone a chance to be included. As another way to facilitate greater involvement in community decision making, since everyone knows each other to some degree, members can usually vote by phone or use a proxy. The community's morale and confidence in the decisions the group makes are always strongest when rolls show that nearly everyone who was eligible participated.

Businesses and Employment

Since the time of The Changeover, all adult members have been responsible for their own income and for the support of their families. Approximately two-thirds of our members and residents work at businesses inside the community or are self-employed, while the remaining third travel to jobs outside the community, primarily in the fields of health care and construction.

The most successful business operating inside The Farm is SE International, the electronics manufacturing firm originally started by The Farm's Radio Crew. The company produces Geiger counters, small handheld devices that detect and monitor exposure to nuclear radiation. Established in the late 1970s, following the near meltdown of the Three Mile Island nuclear plant in Pennsylvania, the company has seen the demand for its products increase exponentially following each worldwide nuclear disaster. The company is run and staffed by a good mix of members from the founding generation and younger people. There's a strong family connection in the social dynamic at SEI, as over the years the company has employed husbands and wives, brothers, sisters, sons, and daughters. Many friendships among the workers there go back more than thirty years.

The Book Publishing Company (BPC) is comparable to SE International in many ways, including the makeup of its personnel. BPC was The Farm's original business, created to publish books by the community founder, Stephen Gaskin. As far back as the early 1970s, the company published several successful titles based on experiences taking place within The Farm. *Spiritual Midwifery*, a compilation of stories about the natural birth experiences of mothers on the early Farm, and including information on prenatal care and childbirth, was originally published more than thirty years ago by Ina May Gaskin and The Farm Midwives. Now in its fourth edition, this book has sold over half a million copies, has been translated into more than a dozen languages, and continues to be a worldwide best seller. *The Farm Vegetarian Cookbook*, a collection of recipes related to The Farm's original vegan lifestyle, also sold well and continues to be part of the company's catalog of titles. The success of this book led to the production of other cookbooks advocating a vegetarian diet and healthy lifestyle, and this has become the company's primary focus. The Book Publishing Company also created a separate imprint called *Native Voices* to publish works by Native American authors and subjects related to their way of life. This niche field grew from relationships established during the initial work by The Farm's nonprofit Plenty International, and it has blossomed as connections with indigenous people in the United States and abroad have grown stronger.

Both SE International and the Book Publishing Company represent successful businesses based in a rural location that use attendance at trade shows as their primary form of marketing. Representatives from each company will travel to a show, set up a professional display, take orders, and make connections, returning to their offices on The Farm to do follow-up and pursue sales leads. It has proven to be an effective way to do business from a rural base.

More on Nonprofits

It has been said that The Farm has more nonprofits per square mile than just about anywhere else in the country. Several provide the primary means of employment for members of the community. Others are managed by volunteers but may use paid staff or Farm residents as subcontractors to perform certain tasks.

The Farm Midwifery Center serves as an umbrella for a number of women in the community who are midwives. Ina May Gaskin has written several successful books about childbirth and babies, and she and the other Farm Midwives have been featured in documentaries that have been shown nationally in theaters and are available on video. The highly regarded Farm Midwifery Center and Midwives attract expectant mothers from around the world seeking their assistance. Besides helping women give birth and publishing books on the subject, The Farm Midwives derive supplemental income by hosting weeklong educational workshops for birthing assistants and aspiring midwives, and they offer advanced classes for professional and certified midwives.

The Farm School is a private school organized as a nonprofit, providing employment for teachers and staff. Typically about half of its registered students come from outside the community, as many parents who live in the area want to take advantage of The Farm School's emphasis on nonviolence, nature, creativity, and self-directed education.

Swan Conservation Trust was formed in 1994 to save a vast forest surrounding The Farm community from being clear-cut by multinational timber interests—a scenario that has befallen thousands and thousands of acres in middle Tennessee over the last thirty years. The fourteen-hundred-acre Big Swan Headwaters Preserve was created in 2004 at a cost of over one million dollars. Money for this preservation project was raised the old-fashioned way: by grassroots appeals and with the assistance of a few small grants. Founded by Farm members, this organization's all-volunteer board and network of support has expanded to include environmentalists and concerned citizens from across the region.

The Advantage of Size

When compared with other intentional communities, the significantly larger population of The Farm community presents several advantages specifically related to employment. The Farm Store is a prime example. Although a small percentage of its customers are people who come from outside, its core constituency and the foundation of its business are the members and residents of the community. Because enough of the community's population shops at The Farm Store, it is a thriving concern and is able to provide full- and part-time employment for several people. Large events, such as conferences and the annual family reunion, help boost its profits. These sales are also directly related to the store's location inside The Farm.

A number of members provide services in demand by people living in the community. People with construction skills, such as framers, electricians, and plumbers, often build additions or perform maintenance to structures on The Farm. Contractors in the community may manage and oversee the building of new homes.

There is always a need for manual labor, and this can be a good way for a young person or someone new to the community to generate some quick income. To make a living by providing a basic service, such as housecleaning, it's helpful to have a sizable population of potential customers, and that's something The Farm has to offer. The flow of money within The Farm's internal economy is a significant element of its success and longevity.

Housing and Green Construction

The community has come a long way since the days of buses and tents. After The Changeover, members of The Farm were able to invest the money they earned to improve their homes. This was a tall order, as many of the large structures that had once provided communal housing for up to forty people had now become single-family homes. Virtually all of these structures needed renovation and have required a sizable investment to cover the cost of upgrades, such as the installation of new roofs, doors and windows; proper flooring; toilets and drain fields; new or updated electrical wiring; and the list goes on. In most instances, at the time of The Changeover, even the interior walls needed to be finished and painted.

With all the homes built during The Farm's communal period occupied by those who stayed after The Changeover, most returning former members and new people joining the community have had to start from scratch, and they've built all types of new homes for themselves. In spite of the housing bubble crash elsewhere in the country, since the new millennium, there's been a housing boom at The Farm. This is even more remarkable considering that all homes on The Farm are built without bank financing.

Because the land of The Farm community is preserved in a trust, home ownership rests with the community, not the individual. All buildings attached to a piece of land are considered part of that land. In this way, all homes on The Farm are owned by a trust created to preserve the land and all other assets in perpetuity for the benefit of current and future Farm members.

The community recognizes that its members have made considerably large capital investments in their homes and acknowledges that this equity has value. Members are permitted to transfer or sell that equity to other members or provisional members through a contract brokered by The Foundation, the corporation that manages all of the community assets owned by the trust. Despite this provision, few people have the cash savings at their disposal to buy out a family's or individual's equity, which can be $100,000 or more.

Banks won't finance transactions on The Farm because our arrangement precludes a banker from selling a home whose owners default on their loan. To sponsor a loan for a home buyer, the community would need to use its land as collateral, and it's unwilling to do that. The Land Trust document prohibits the land from being encumbered or endangered in any way.

The housing situation is both a strength and a weakness for the community. On the one hand, people who live on The Farm are mortgage-free. A bank cannot come in to evict or take away a family's home if an illness or some other misfortune disrupts their income. At the same time, the absence of bank financing may prevent people who have limited funds from joining the community or building a new home on The Farm.

Despite this hurdle, in any given year it is not uncommon to see four or five new homes under construction on The Farm. Sometimes people coming into the community have sold a home on the outside and use the profit to build on The Farm. Others may spend years saving money to build, or they may use inherited money for that purpose. Many will start out with a small cabin and then add on as they save more money, a pay-as-you-go plan. Those with construction skills, who are able to function as contractors and do much of the labor themselves, have a particular advantage.

The people who fall into one of the scenarios described above often tend to be folks who moved to The Farm after retirement, or they are people who have solid incomes. Young families just starting out seem to have a tougher time arranging for new housing on The Farm, as they bear the expense of raising children, have little savings, and are less likely to have achieved their peak earning potential.

Occasionally, the community is able to provide small loans to help someone get through a certain phase of construction. Once the loan has been repaid, the borrower can usually apply again—another version of the pay-as-you-go plan.

The homes built during the communal period in the 1970s were constructed primarily from recycled building materials acquired through demolition and salvage operations; and, of course, they were built without concern for paying workers' wages. Now that the cost of labor must be factored in, that type of work is no longer cost-effective. Still, if anything, The Farm is a place for idealists, and the construction of a home becomes a way to express core values of sustainability and energy efficiency that can be emulated by society at large. Because members invest their own money when they build, each home is a reflection of choices made by the homeowners, based on their budget, personal desires, compromises, and priorities.

Green building is about energy efficiency. White enamel-coated tin, with an estimated life span of forty years, reflects light in the sun's heat—even infrared rays—and can help keep a home cool, which is especially important in the hot climate of Tennessee. Spray foam insulation creates a tight seal and offers a high degree of energy efficiency. Homes built from insulated concrete forms, or ICFs, are extremely energy efficient, with the superinsulation of a double wall of foam sandwiching poured concrete, creating massive walls that will resist the mightiest tornado, another consideration in the region. As we look ahead to the possibility of increasingly powerful storms caused by climate change, it makes sense to build with ICFs.

Cement board siding is virtually indestructible. Some have used siding from cypress boards that are rustic and attractive as well as naturally resistant to rot and bugs. Others prefer siding from locally harvested poplar, a fast-growing tree and a renewable resource.

Natural builders work with materials such as straw and clay, and round log poles for framing and post and beam construction. The mixture of straw and clay provides insulation and a strong foundation to support natural earth plasters that coat the interior and exterior walls. This allows the interior rooms to "breathe" and transfer humidity, a natural cooling technique that eliminates the need for air conditioning. Standard roofing materials, such as tin and shingles, are replaced with "living roofs," a surface covered entirely by grasses and plants, which provide both insulation and a method for natural cooling.

These represent but a few examples of materials and techniques that have been used to build new homes in the community after The Changeover. This dedication to sustainable principles is one of the more visible examples that visitors might encounter at The Farm. With all of the homes set into or nestled along the edge of the forest, The Farm's housing is in sync with the fundamental principles of permaculture, life integrated with nature.

Ethnic Diversity

When examining The Farm's population and demographics, it's impossible to miss the fact that the community has very little ethnic diversity. This is a direct result of the cultural phenomenon responsible for The Farm's very existence. The hippie movement emerged when a segment of the baby boomer generation, predominantly white middle-class kids, rebelled against the materialistic values of their parents and society. This was taken to another level on The Farm when members signed a Vow of Poverty, a commitment in direct conflict with the country's African American population seeking to escape the yoke of poverty that had become, for many, a cultural legacy. While in the 1960s and 1970s, people of color were actively engaged in a struggle to live, work, earn, and spend as their white peers did, people joining The Farm were rejecting the very status and privilege this segment of America sought to achieve.

Throughout The Farm community's history, a few people of color have made The Farm their home for some period of time, but for numerous reasons, they have chosen to move on. Consequently, the overall population remains a mix of predominantly Western European ethnicities.

The Farm's location in the rural South has also played a role in affecting its ethnic diversity. The blatant racism associated with the South, depicted in films and other media, is based on realities that continue to lurk in the shadows. Soon after the buses arrived in Lewis County, we learned it was commonly known that it was unwise for a black person to remain in Summertown after dark. I remember coming upon signs indicating the separate "colored" and "white" bathrooms in a gas station at a nearby town. Although the signs were no longer in use, they were a stark reminder of the past and the attitudes that still can occasionally rise to the surface. Although much has changed over the last forty years, it's clear that the roots of racism are slow to die in our society and that African Americans shoulder an extra burden when choosing to settle in the midst of redneck culture in a "red state."

The reality of community is also that people feel most comfortable when surrounded by people who share their cultural values, experiences, and background. New people drawn to The Farm in the present day are responding to the same urges that were at the original roots of the hippie counterculture: a rejection of urban existence, a return to simplicity, and a lifestyle more in tune with nature.

Stephen and Ina May Gaskin

It is significant to note that The Farm is one of the few social experiments in which even after power shifted away from the original charismatic leader, that person stayed and lived among the group as an ordinary member. Although he was unhappy about the turn of events at the time of The Changeover, Stephen stayed on The Farm. The decade of the 1980s was a period of introspection for Stephen and Ina May, as it was for everyone else who had been living at The Farm. It was, for all of us, a time to reflect on the wild ride that had finally come to an end.

The decision to stay on was made somewhat easier for the Gaskins by the fact that Stephen and Ina May's home was in a secluded location at the end of a road that had no other houses. They were able to retreat to the woods and move on with their personal lives in privacy.

Although their status in the community had diminished, the Gaskins never lost their renown as counterculture celebrities. Stephen was occasionally called upon for speaking engagements, and in 2000 he was one of the candidates to be the Green Party's nominee for president. He wasn't chosen as the Green Party's candidate, but this political gambit gave

Stephen an excuse to go on the road speaking to crowds large and small that were receptive to his message, essentially a left-of-center view of world affairs with a platform of universal health care, campaign finance reform, and the legalization of marijuana.

Ina May has spent the last several decades furthering her reputation as the primary spokesperson for midwifery. Relying on her early experience in this field and her education as an English major, she authored several more books on childbirth and early childhood development. Ina May went on to serve as president of the Midwife Alliance of North America (MANA) from 1996 to 2002, spending much of her time traveling to speaking engagements at midwifery conferences around the country and throughout the world.

A technique Ina May learned from a Guatemalan midwife as a solution for shoulder dystocia, a condition in which a baby's head is delivered but the shoulders are stuck inside the mother's body during the birth process, was officially named The Gaskin Maneuver by the medical establishment, further cementing her reputation. Her work on behalf of women and the sanctity of birth was recognized in 2009 when she received an honorary doctorate from the Thames Valley University of London, England. Two years later, Ina May received the prestigious Right Livelihood Award, known as an alternative to the Nobel Prize and presented by the Swedish Parliament. The award came with special meaning for Ina May: Stephen was one of the inaugural recipients of the Right Livelihood Award in 1980, when he was recognized for founding Plenty International, The Farm's relief and development organization. In addition to honoring them as individuals, the awards are a validation of The Farm's work over the last forty years on behalf of human rights at many different levels.

New Voices

It wasn't until the turn of the century that we began seeing the return of children who had been born on The Farm but had left for college or other pursuits. When these young people come back to settle down, there's usually a good chance the move coincides with finding a mate, a partner also looking to put down roots. It's a phenomenon that echoes the cycle of life found in other tribal and rural societies. When considering where to have children and raise a family, these new parents recognize that their own experience growing up on The Farm was something very precious and they want to pass that on to the next generation. Taking this step means they will need their own housing, instead of moving back in with their folks, an important step forward for this next generation.

Typically the young people who never left, as well as those who left but returned to establish a home, had parents who remained in the community after The Changeover. As a result, the generation now poised to inherit The Farm has several advantages that were not available to The Farm's founding members. In contrast to the situation with The Farm's original settlers, the ideological gap between parents and their grown children is not that wide, and the two age groups hold many common ideals. Another boon for The Farm's next generation of parents is that they can take advantage of support from grandparents close at hand. And, with a sympathetic bond between the generations, the advice of these elders is highly regarded by this new group of young people. They are receptive to mentoring by the older generation, and they may also benefit from inheriting access to work, as their elders have established some strong, functioning businesses for their children to step into.

One of the community's great strengths is the shared appreciation for music and the similar musical tastes that span all generations. Typical Farm parties include people of all ages rocking out together. Not surprisingly, musicianship is one aspect of Farm life that has successfully been passed on from one generation to the next. Multiple bands have been spawned from the children of founding members, providing the entertainment at countless events.

The vision of a sustainable future, with people living together cooperatively, is being expressed by a new set of voices that represent The Farm today. To be sure, there will be new ideas and innovative projects from this homegrown wave of responsible, idealistic adults who, along with their peers, have been drawn to make The New Farm their home.

Biko was born in Ireland. His parents had met and married on The Farm and then departed for Europe in the late 1970s to start a satellite community. They returned when he was three, and he grew up on The Farm, but Biko left when he reached his early twenties. "When I graduated high school, I joined The Construction Crew and worked full-time. As soon as I had enough money, I bounced out and went to South Africa. I had learned about natural building and permaculture at the Ecovillage Training Center, and I went to South Africa to further that knowledge. I also traveled to India and Sri Lanka and participated in a large conference about the development of ecovillages.

"Upon returning, I came to truly realize how precious it is to have this land and how precious it is to have community. I better understand how fortunate we are to have the knowledge and technology that is here.

"When you think about it, you have this whole piece of land that was the vision of the founding generation, and then you have an entire generation that was born on the land and grew up in that. The questions become: What do those people feel about that land? What are their ideas? What is their vision? I would say we are trying to continue the vision of The Farm forward and honor the roots of our parents' values, but we also want to go beyond that and to use the new knowledge and wisdom that's available to us now. I feel like nurturing the roots is so important in this day and age, and it is so easy to always be looking for the greener pastures. I feel a certain sense of responsibility, you know. I have been given so much. I mean even how my parents fed me and took care of me. I want to give back. I have a lot of faith in the next generation, the young kids that are growing up now. They are getting the best of everything the previous two generations have learned."

Alayne and her husband, Jason, grew up on the East Coast with no family ties to hippie culture. It wasn't until they left home and found each other that they began to express an affinity with New Age philosophy and alternative lifestyles. They were attracted to The Farm for many reasons, not the least of which was Alayne's desire to live in a place that supported natural childbirth. "The allopathic model of the hospital did not resonate with me," Alayne explains. "We came to meet with The Midwives and liked the energy of the women here, and the men too! It really surprised me that the men of the community were just as supportive and excited about the impending birth as we were. We were looking around and wanted to live in a close-knit community. We liked The Farm because it was child-centered, it was family-oriented. The emphasis on sustainability and outreach as expressed by things like the Ecovillage Training Center were also a draw for us." Jason added, "It was just what we were looking for."

Tierra was born on The Farm but left when her parents moved away around the time of The Changeover. She returned at the age of fourteen, when her mother moved back, spending her teenage years and transition to adulthood as part of The New Farm. "Being part of the next generation is exciting and a privilege and has afforded so many opportunities," Tierra said. "But it also involves responsibilities that I think many of us are just beginning to realize. There is a great need for more of the next generation to be a part of this community. In doing that, we need to pinpoint who we are and have a strong sense of identity and a sense of purpose about what we want to create here. I think that is our biggest challenge."

Mark was born on The Farm and now lives with his wife and child in the home that was once occupied by his parents. "I view The Farm as a large extended family and a soul tribe, a group of people who have chosen on a conscious, spiritual level to come together and be a tribal people, an indigenous type of culture for our day and age.

"I notice this even more when I travel out in the greater society that is driven so much by production and consumption. Everything and everyone is focused on consuming, consuming, consuming, and what product are they going to purchase next to feel good about themselves or buy in order to make their reality a little bit better. In contrast, our life here on The Farm is centered around community. What time can we spend together? How can we enrich each other's lives? There is an interconnection that holds it all together."

One of the biggest challenges facing the generation that will inherit The Farm community is how to increase their numbers, so that in the future they will have enough members with incomes sufficient to share the costs for operating and maintaining the community. As this is being written, approximately two-thirds of The Farm's members are from the founding generation. Most are still working and earning an income. As the founding members age and move into retirement, with fixed or lower incomes, their ability to pay toward the community's monthly dues is likely to diminish and the burden of funding the community's annual budget will be shouldered by a progressively smaller group. Unless the succeeding generation is able to increase its numbers or develop a way for the community itself to generate income to cover costs, such as paying annual land taxes, operating the water system, maintaining roads and public buildings, and a host of other items, every individual will bear an increasingly larger portion of the budget.

The End of the Road

For a good number of family and friends, The Farm Cemetery is the last stop on their journey. Some people buried there are the parents of founding members who came to live in the community for their final days. There are also a number of graves for souls who did not survive birth or died during childhood. Every marker represents a story, a history, and a connection to the land. Quite often people who have spent any significant amount of time in the community and were affected deeply by their experience choose to return and be buried here. It is sacred ground.

On an evening close to or on Halloween, community members will gather at The Farm Cemetery to honor the dead, following a tradition common in Latin American countries. All Souls Day is said to represent the thinnest veil between the living and the departed. As day turns into night, a lit candle inside a brown paper sack is placed on each grave. The flickering glow provides an eerie but warm reminder that we are not alone; we carry the memories of our loved ones in our hearts and minds. On this night, around a fire, we share stories of those who've gone before us.

The Land

When the land was first purchased, our communal agreement about its ownership was above and beyond paper titles. It was about a bond and a commitment everyone shared as a spiritual community. It was our belief that any one of us could own the land and hold it in trust for The Farm Church, for all of us. And that is kind of how it worked. A few folks were asked to put their names on the deed. That served us for about forty years. Over time, one name or another on the deed has changed, and other core members of the community have been chosen to hold the land in their names. Deborah was asked at some point in the mid-1980s to put her name on the deed, and she served as a trustee for twenty-five years.

This type of ownership is known as a common-law trust, recognized in Tennessee by our years here on the land. But to protect the land in perpetuity, as whole and forever undivided, and for it to remain a symbol of the energy that came together in a great pure effort, we needed to produce a stronger legal document, something that spelled out the ownership of the land. We needed a trust.

It took us ten years to define, refine, and craft the descriptive statements, define the purpose of our land trust, and detail who we are as beneficiaries. The trust recognizes that we are stewards and that we feel a relationship with and responsibility to nature, the ultimate owner of this land. The trust acknowledges the greater tribe of The Farm community, for whom this land holds special meaning.

Beyond the Borders

The sense of community embodied by The Farm extends beyond its immediate borders. A growing number of people affiliated with the community choose to live nearby rather than within it. In this way, they can remain autonomous and still derive the benefits of the community. The New

Farm recognizes the valuable contributions these folks bring with them, such as participation and support for The Farm School and other nonprofits, a variety of skills, and a desire to grow the regional network of like-minded people.

Douglas and Deborah.

This number includes my daughter and son-in-law, who moved back to The Farm for a number of years before purchasing a beautiful home on twenty-five acres a few miles down the road. Living nearby enables us to stay connected and help each other and play active roles in our shared lives, such as our babysitting the grandkids and their assisting in the care of my elderly mother when she moved to The Farm. At the same time, they have space and independence apart from the social complexities of life in community. I am so thankful and grateful for their presence in my life.

The many hundreds of people who have shared The Farm experience continue to stay connected as a greater tribe. Large contingencies of former Farmees can be found here and there across the nation, often working together in business or for social causes or just gathering for fun at small get-togethers or large reunions. The digital network of social media has made it possible to renew and maintain friendships, post family updates, foster lighthearted conversations, and even engage in debates. Right livelihood, work that expresses The Farm's ideals, continues to be a common thread in the chosen professions of the former members and in the children of former and current residents who have absorbed the spiritual principles and now express them in their own ways.

In that regard, I am proud to say my son is a great example. He lives with his wife and their daughter in Asheville, North Carolina, a hip town in the mountains about six hours from The Farm. It's a place where a large number of the children who grew up here in Tennessee, as well as a number of former founding members, have chosen to settle. My son started out teaching immigrants for whom English was a second language. He now oversees a program that provides training and helps find employment for people coming out of the prison system.

It has been a full and interesting life, and I'm so grateful for Deborah's strength and love that have carried us through. My wife and I share a bond with our children that goes beyond anything we could have imagined when we arrived at The Farm as mere teenagers. To my mind it speaks to the true nature of sustainability, which is not just about solar panels or growing food, but how we pass on our values to the next generations. It is important to take time away from our self-important busy lives to nurture our world's most precious resource, our children, who are the only true path to the future.

The Farm Is a State of Mind

Technically The Farm is a physical place, a dot on the map. The reality is that The Farm is a gestalt entity, a whole created by the sum of its parts, and it remains true that its most vital elements are created by the relationships that connect and extend from person to person to person. The Farm has the unique ability to touch something deep within the human soul, and it leaves an everlasting imprint on anyone who has visited for a day or for a week, or who has lived there for months or for years or has never left.

The open fields and forested ridges that encompass our land are a symbol of the dream all people have of a better way, a dream of humans living together in harmony with each other and with nature, where peace is a priority, not a luxury.

The Farm has never been and never will be perfect. It mirrors the human experience, the cycles of life that include every type of human drama and shortcoming, including all the failures and mistakes, frustrations and disappointments we feel when we fall short of our ideals. As is the way of the universe, the yin and the yang, these negative elements are balanced by the joy, the laughter, and the love emanating from every beating heart.

This is why as a community we are at our best and most blessed when our members include people of all ages, from the newborn to the aged. Both can serve as living examples of innocence, a purity that reminds us every day of the sacredness of life. They inspire us to do better, to appreciate what we have, and to do what we can for those in need.

How long will The Farm exist? How long will people live on this land as a community? Only time can answer that. But I believe, even more than hope, that the energy that has called every person here to this place will continue to work its magic . . . for generations to come.

About the Author

For over forty years, Douglas Stevenson has lived and worked on the cutting edge of alternative lifestyles and technology. Although his work has taken him around the world, his home base is a log cabin out in the woods, surrounded by nature.

Douglas is the media interface and principal spokesperson for The Farm, once a hippie commune, now the largest and most famous intentional community in the world, a living example and model for a sustainable lifestyle. His interviews have appeared in countless newspaper and magazine articles, documentaries, and TV news programs, such as CNN's *Making It In America*.

In 1981 he started Village Media, a business that provides video, web, and other communication services for companies and nonprofits throughout the United States. Its web presence can be found at villagemedia.com. For the last ten years, Douglas has been the host of Green Life Retreats, which sponsors educational workshops, conferences, small festivals, and other events promoting the green lifestyle—a way of living that combines technology and respect for nature, sustainability, and community. More information is available at greenliferetreats.com.

Douglas is the author of three previous books and has written more than one thousand articles that have appeared in a variety of national and international magazines. He travels to schools, universities, and events, where he is a sought-after speaker on the topics of sustainability, responsible stewardship of the earth, alternative lifestyles, and building with respect for nature. Visit Douglas at douglasstevenson.com.

Sacred Land: The land of The Farm is held in a trust, preserved in perpetuity for future generations.

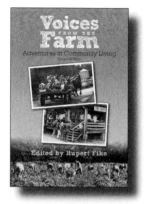